INTRODUCTION TO POLITICS

Introduction to Politics

DOROTHY M. PICKLES

Methuen & Co Ltd

For the students of Morley College
with whom most of the subjects
dealt with in this book have been
thrashed out in amiable discussion.

First published 1951 by the Sylvan Press

First published in this series (revised edition) 1964
Reprinted three times
Reprinted with corrections 1976
Reprinted 1977

Printed and bound in Great Britain by
J. W. Arrowsmith Ltd, Bristol

ISBN 0 416 68690 7

Distributed in the U.S.A. by
HARPER & ROW PUBLISHERS, INC.
BARNES & NOBLE IMPORT DIVISION

Table of Contents

PREFACE   ix

Part I : Man and the State

CHAPTER 1   IS MAN A POLITICAL ANIMAL ?   15

Permanence of the quest for the " good life"; the relation of the political scientist to politics—its remoteness from his control and the extent to which he is a part of the process that he is analysing; the influence of environment and national character; why we ought to study politics; the extent to which politics is, or can be, a science; the contribution of history to an understanding of politics; how the study of politics can improve the quality of citizenship.

CHAPTER 2   THE PROBLEM OF POWER IN THE STATE   34

The State, the Government and the Nation; The State as Power and the extent to which its use of power is, or can be, modified in practice. *The problem of sovereignty* :—legal and political sovereignty; popular sovereignty and the ultimate control of the nation; the difficulties of achieving popular sovereignty in practice; the difficulty of defining sovereignty.

The effective limitations of State power :—limitations due to history and tradition; limitations imposed by the need to secure assent; methods by which the State seeks to secure assent; the influence of political evolution on contemporary attitudes; the relation between the State and groups within the State; the special position of religious and political associations; the difficulty of finding a general definition of the desirable limits of State action and individual freedom.

CHAPTER 3   THE PROBLEM OF OBEDIENCE   57

Why do we obey the State? The influence of force, religion, habit and tradition in making up men's minds on the subject of obedience; the concept of a social contract; its importance in the seventeenth century; different theories regarding the nature of the contract; the questions that the contract theory leaves unanswered; Rousseau's Social Contract and the difficulty of translating its ideals into practice; the theory of the general will; the difficulties of expressing the community spirit in political institutions; the individualism of Jeremy Bentham; over-simplifications of the nineteenth-century Utilitarian attitude; twentieth-century uncertainties and the problem of minorities.

CHAPTER 4   THE PROBLEM OF CHANGE   84
What we mean by revolution; what makes people rebel; the
dangers of revolution; the moral argument against revolution; the
problem of revolutionary minorities in a democracy; the value and
the difficulty of compromise; the dilemma of the toleration of
intolerance.
The democratic alternative to revolution, and why the Marxists
reject it; examples of change during the past century; modern
democratic attitudes to the problem of change—technocratic,
functional and Fabian solutions.

CHAPTER 5   THE STATE IN RELATION TO OTHER
                    STATES   109
The growth of internationalism; the weaknesses of the League
as an instrument for preventing war; the difficulty of harmonizing
long-run and short-run national interests; the failure to establish
confidence in the stability of international institutions; the growth
of practical international solidarity; the value and limitations of
functional international institutions; national change in an interdependent world; ideological obstacles to internationalism; differing
views on how war can be prevented; the movement for European
integration.

Part II : Man and his Fellow Citizens

CHAPTER 6   MAN AS A SOCIAL ANIMAL   137
The citizen's problem as a little man in a big world; the need
for wider opportunities of citizenship; the importance of local and
professional interests; the possibility of new techniques of consultation; the State as the guarantor of fundamental rights.

CHAPTER 7   THE FUNDAMENTAL RIGHTS OF THE
                    CITIZEN   150
Moral or natural rights; the eighteenth-century attitude to rights
as exemplified by the American Declaration of Independence and
the French *Déclaration des Droits de l'Homme et du Citoyen*; Locke
and natural rights; the modern attitude to fundamental rights as
exemplified by the Universal Declaration of Human Rights;
changes in conceptions of fundamental rights and differences of
practical application; the essential subjectivity of the concept of
natural rights.
Constitutional rights; difficulties in enforcing constitutional
rights; the value and limitations of constitutional rights; the
attempt to provide a European guarantee of human rights in the
form of a European Convention; the difficulties encountered in
applying the Convention; the practical problems of relating rights
and duties.

CHAPTER 8   RIGHTS   AND   DUTIES   IN   A   MODERN
                         DEMOCRACY   175
Changing concepts of rights during the past century; how they
have increased the dependence of the citizen on the State and complicated the problem of relating rights to duties; some of the
implications of recognizing a right to work; the value of the
affirmation of principle; the inter-relationship of rights; some
examples of changes in the attitude towards other rights as a result
of the changing attitude to social welfare; some implications of the
right to social welfare; the moral responsibility of the citizen.

CHAPTER 9   LIBERTY AND EQUALITY   198
Rights as the means to the attainment of liberty; the concept of
liberty influenced by attitudes towards equality and towards the
relation of means and ends; the Marxist and democratic approaches
to liberty; John Stuart Mill on liberty; more and less optimistic
assumptions in the twentieth century; interpretations of the right
to equality; equality and property; over-emphasis of certain
aspects of equality as a hindrance to liberty; the meaning of equality
of opportunity and the difficulty of achieving it; doubts as to
whether it can or ought to be achieved; Bernard Shaw's interpretation of it as equality of income; the case for trying to achieve it and
for believing that it may not be incompatible with liberty.

APPENDIX   LIST OF BOOKS FOR FURTHER READING   218

INDEX   221

Preface

THIS book has three aims. It seeks, first, to stimulate thought
and discussion on those problems of present-day politics which
are permanent subjects of political enquiry. The method which
has been adopted is, therefore, one that asks questions rather
than suggests answers. If the present generation of students
seems to many of us less interested in politics—or perhaps
more disillusioned about them—than was the last post-war
generation, I believe that it is largely owing to the complexity
and confusion of our contemporary political scene, which
tempts people either to grasp too easily at answers, without
first asking the appropriate questions, or else to assume too
readily that there are no sensible answers. The difficulty of
persuading them to ask questions and to face the somewhat
bleak prospect of having to base provisional conclusions on no
less provisional hypotheses, as a preferable alternative to either
dogma or escapism, can, however, be overcome. Once students
realize that the problems of other times often looked to those
who had to deal with them as complex and apparently insoluble as ours do to us, and that if we learn to make allowances
for differences of vocabulary, of economic or political habits,
or of emphasis, we can recognize in them problems essentially
similar to those with which we are trying to grapple, then
much of their discouragement disappears.

To the extent that this approach succeeds in interesting
students both in the problems themselves and in the different
ways in which men of other times or other countries have tried
to solve them, two aims will have been achieved. Students
will ask questions and try to work out the answers for
themselves; and they will want to study more closely the works
of authors whose opinions have been summarized or merely

mentioned. Experience of teaching politics and political ideas
has convinced me that it is often useless to try to persuade
students who have not had much academic training to tackle
whole slabs of classical, or even of comparatively modern,
writing on these subjects. The style and vocabulary, as well as
the background, are too unfamiliar for them to follow the
argument with real interest. Once they become familiar with,
and interested in, the problems at issue, they will read anything and everything on them, provided they know where to
start and, roughly, what to expect.

If this conclusion is accurate, then it is essential that a book
of this type should also provide the necessary introduction to
such further reading. This is its third aim. A guide to further
reading has, therefore, been given in the appendix. It en-
deavours to make it easy for the student to carry on from the
point at which the book leaves off. Where a quotation has
either not been acknowledged in the text, or has been accompanied by the name of the author, without the page reference,
it can easily be traced to its source in one of the books included
in the list dealing with that particular subject in the appendix.
An introductory study ought not to be encumbered with
footnotes. On the other hand, nothing is more infuriating than
to be unable to locate an attractive or illuminating quotation.
I hope that this solution will prevent annoyance on either
score.

I should like to add two personal notes. The first is in the
nature of a warning or an apology. The method adopted has
involved frequent references to and quotations from the works
of writers who have made important contributions to the
history of political thought. Little or no attempt has been
made, however, to consider either the individuals or their
ideas as a whole or in relation to their time. The inevitable
result is that there are over-simplifications, omissions, and, at
times, distortions. In mitigation of the offence, may I emphasize that this is not intended to be in any sense a text-book on
political thought, but merely, as the title states, an intro-

duction to some fundamental problems of contemporary politics.

The second is an acknowledgment. I should like to take this opportunity of expressing my gratitude to two of my teachers: to Professor R. H. Soltau, formerly of the London School of Economics, who first aroused my interest in politics, and particularly in French politics; and to the late Harold Laski, to whose teaching, writings, personal influence and great kindness, I, like thousands of other students of political science, shall be eternally indebted. He would not have agreed with everything that I have said in this book. But I hope that he would have recognized in it an honest attempt to think out the implications of political assumptions, as he always encouraged his students to do.

D. M. P.

London, 1950.

THE thirteen years since the publication of the first edition of this book have seen some astounding changes in the political, economic and strategic fields. I have, therefore, rewritten sections that have gone out of date, or become less relevant to current preoccupations, taking account as far as space allowed of new problems and new attitudes. On some points I have changed my own mind. Where I have felt that opinions or summaries of the views of political thinkers were inaccurately expressed, I have rewritten the passages, I hope more carefully. I should have liked to include references to a number of views expressed since I wrote—and notably to those of Professors Michael Oakeshott, J. D. B. Miller, and Bernard Crick. For practical reasons, I have been able to do no more than include what seem to me the most relevant of these in the guide to further reading, which has been largely recast.

Some readers may feel that, in the circumstances, I should have rewritten the book entirely, and it is true that if I were to write an introduction to politics today, I should write it quite differently. But I have kept the basic framework because I have no reason to feel that anything that has happened since the appearance of the first edition has invalidated the case for a book of this kind. It was written, as I have said, in response to the specific needs of particular students. It is because I felt then, and still feel, that these needs were and are those of a much wider audience that I have left so much of it unchanged.

DOROTHY PICKLES

1964.

THE thirteen years since the publication of the last revised edition have seen even more extensive and more profound political changes. In revising the book once again, I have followed a similar procedure to that adopted last time, taking account of important changes of emphasis or attitudes, where I could, and including brief references to those events whose impact seems peculiarly relevant to the problems discussed. I have also revised the bibliography in order to include, along with the basic background studies, a few of the more recent books that might appeal especially to the type of student that I had in mind when I wrote the book.

DOROTHY PICKLES

1976.

PART ONE

Man and the State

CHAPTER ONE

Is Man a Political Animal?

THE practice of politics is necessarily as old as society itself. Wherever men live in a community, they must accept certain rules of conduct, if only to safeguard the existence of the community itself and to prevent some members of it from killing others. The rules governing a society may be few or many. They can range from a few primitive traditions, handed down orally from one generation to another, to the whole complex set of constitutional and governmental regulations which we associate with the modern State.

The study of politics, which is sometimes called political science, is born when men begin to speculate about the rules by which they are governed, or by which their ancestors were governed, when they begin to ask whether these rules ought to be accepted, or ought to have been accepted in the past, why some societies choose different rules from others, whether it is possible to find the best rules for a particular society, or whether it is possible to discover general rules of conduct which could, or should, be applicable to all societies. In order to answer these questions, they are obliged to make more fundamental enquiries into the purposes for which human societies exist and their relation to the purpose of human life itself. This enquiry into the purposes of government has been going on for thousands of years, because men have never been able to reach agreed conclusions. Nor is there any likelihood that they ever will do so, for human civilizations are forever changing and what seems true, and even self-evident, for one generation or one civilization is frequently rejected by others. Each generation, as it becomes adult, is faced with the responsibility of deciding whether to accept the rules made or accepted by earlier generations, or whether to challenge their validity and try to replace them by others. The ordinary citizen, trying to make up his mind whether to vote for X or Y, may be trying to answer the question which Plato and Aristotle tried to answer over 2,000 years ago, namely: What is the best form of government? Of course, he may not be thinking of these wider issues at all. He may simply be trying to decide whether X or Y is the more likely to further his own personal or professional interests. Even so, he is unconsciously helping to formulate an answer of some kind to the question: What is the best form of government for me? And the thousands of different answers provided by him and by his fellow electors over a period of years go to form the way in which government in a particular country develops. The impact which one individual citizen makes on his own or succeeding generations may be infinitesimally small. It will depend partly on the extent to which he is interested in the problems of politics, partly on his ability to express his views, partly on the opportunities which are available to him to make his opinions known and to the skill and understanding that he brings to the task. It will depend, too, on the element of chance which determines whether the opinions that he expresses are in tune with the spirit of the time in which he lives. Some brilliant political thinkers have failed to influence their contemporaries because their ideas were too far in advance of their time to win support. At any given period of history, most people seem to accept the rules of the society in which they live without giving a thought to the matter, some question their rightness but do nothing about it, some challenge them, but are never able to make their voices heard. At some periods of history, people have been forcibly prevented from making their criticisms, and in totalitarian States, even to-day, criticism of the State seems to be a dangerous adventure. Some critics of society, however, have so touched the minds or hearts of their fellow citizens or of the citizens of other times or other countries, that they have helped to bring about great changes in the organization of government. Plato and Aristotle still influence the thought of Western Europe, after more than 2,000 years. Thinkers like Rousseau and Karl Marx so changed the way people looked at political problems that they set in motion forces whose influence is still being felt far beyond the frontiers of their own countries.

Because we are still unable, after thousands of years, to give final answers to the fundamental questions about how men ought to organize their community life, it does not follow that the study of politics and political ideas is valueless. In any science, the number of propositions which can be accepted unquestioningly at all times and in all places is very small. As far as we know, all attempts to make two plus two equal five have failed, and are likely to do so. Red litmus paper will always turn blue if placed in an alkaline solution and blue will turn red if placed in an acid solution. But the subjects on which the human race has reached that degree of certainty are few and relatively unimportant in comparison with those which are still enveloped in a high degree of uncertainty. Medical scientists can still not tell us with any certainty what causes life or sleep, but they do know a great deal more than they used to know about what makes people ill and what cures them. Their knowledge is perpetually changing, so that one generation may be treated quite differently from another for what is, or appears to be, the same disease. In the same way, the science of politics has taught us a great deal about men and their Governments. Some of the conclusions have persisted for centuries, others have been rejected, others, again are accepted to-day and may be rejected by future generations. Some are still in dispute, being accepted by some people, or nations, and rejected by others.

It is peculiarly difficult for the student of politics to reach conclusions which have either the degree of certainty or the universality of the laws of natural science, partly because he stands in a different relationship to his subject and partly because the subject-matter itself is less easy to define precisely. Political organization and behaviour are so diverse and so complex that any one generation can observe only a very small part of them. They are like an unending film of which we see only a few shots. We have a garbled idea of what happened before we came in—inevitably garbled, because the historians and political thinkers on whom we rely to interpret the past for us have themselves never been able to look at more than a similarly fragmentary extract. But even if we had a complete understanding of the past, it would not give us any certain guidance for the future, because it is never possible to reproduce exactly the political, social or economic conditions which gave rise to any particular form of political behaviour. Nor, indeed, is it possible to know exactly how far particular conditions do, in fact, explain behaviour. All the knowledge that we can accumulate about how men have chosen their rulers and how rulers have maintained or lost their power, about how or why people have rebelled against their leaders, will not enable us to say with any certainty how a different set of people, living at a different time or in a different place, will react to a set of circumstances which, however great the resemblances, can never be exactly the same.

Of course, this kind of uncertainty exists, too, in other sciences. If the political scientist who defines the causes of, say, revolutions, cannot predict in any particular case if, or when, a revolution will break out, whether it will be successful, or what kind of régime will follow it, doctors and psychologists who define the causes of certain individual or social illnesses can often not make much more confident predictions. We are told, for example, that worry and overwork are predisposing factors in the development of gastric ulcers. Yet many worriers do not suffer from ulcers, and it is impossible to predict in any individual case whether an ulcer will or will not develop, when it will do so, how serious it will be, or whether it will respond to treatment. When the elder Pitt said, in 1770, that "unlimited power is apt to corrupt the minds of those who possess it", he was making a statement essentially similar to the statement that worry and overwork are apt to encourage the development of ulcers.

The peculiar difficulties encountered by the political scientist come from his greater closeness to the subject of his study and also, in another sense, from his greater remoteness from it. He is remote from it, in a way in which the natural scientist is not, because he cannot control it. To go back to the analogy between the study of revolutions and gastric ulcers, it is possible for a doctor to control to some extent the behaviour of a number of patients whom he suspects of having ulcers and to compare their reactions to different treatments with those of normal people. The political scientist may be convinced that past policies somewhere, at some time, have led to revolution. He cannot argue on the basis of that conviction that similar policies would necessarily produce the same results if applied anywhere else or at any other time, since he is an onlooker with no control over events. He cannot experiment in revolutions to test his theories, and the chances that the particular kind of revolution which he wants to study will occur more than once in a lifetime are negligible. Indeed, it is never possible for him to be sure that any two revolutions are alike enough to justify more than very tentative comparisons.

The political scientist is closer to his subject than the natural scientist, however, because, although he cannot induce changes, society itself sometimes can. Conditions may change in a way that the political thinker cannot foresee, because either he himself or other thinkers have, by their analysis, taken a hand in determining the trend of future events. In other words, the political scientist may be himself a motive force in the evolution that he and those who follow him are trying to analyse. Karl Marx, writing at a particular moment in the evolution of capitalism, predicted the course of its future development. It may well be that the generations following him changed that course because they wished to prevent the consequences which he had predicted. For example, if British capitalists do not react to Socialist legislation as Marx predicted they would, it may be, in part at least, because he opened their eyes to possible unpleasant consequences and they decided not to risk verifying his hypothesis, but to choose present discomforts instead of possible future catastrophe. It is important to remember also that such a choice need not have been a conscious one. It may have been made as a result of the unconscious absorption of ideas by a society.

Natural scientists are not, to anything like this extent, a part of the process that they are analysing, although they are closer to it than is often supposed. A doctor who conducts experiments, say, to find a cure for measles, will not find that the number of cases that break out varies as a result of his findings, unless it is as a result of definite experiments carried out to test hypotheses. It is never possible to isolate particular influences going to make up the stream of the historical process with the degree of exactness with which the medical scientist can isolate this or that symptom of a particular disease. "You cannot", as R. H. S. Crossman has said, "remove a little slice of life called politics or a slab of organization called the state from the intricate structure of human society and hope to understand it." We cannot even attribute this or that political development to the influence of this or that political thinker. We can be fairly certain that his views have played some part, along with other complex forces, but we cannot work out exactly how important his contribution is. We do know that the appeal of certain thinkers owes much to interpretations of their ideas which are often misinterpretations. For example, it is often argued that Karl Marx would not have accepted all the ideas of modern Marxists. And the ideas of Jesus Christ have given rise to a bewildering number of different versions of Christianity. We still know comparatively little of the processes by which political societies learn to adopt new ideas. When it happens, we are too close to it all,

too much a small part of a complex and large-scale development, to be able to see what is happening in its proper
perspective. By the time we are able to get things into focus
they have become part of history.

The political scientist is inseparable from his subject, not
only because he is a part of it and as such is helping to make
up the stream of its future development, but also because he
is a product of it. He cannot look at it from outside, because
he sees what is happening through the spectacles of his own
particular environment. As a member of the society whose
purposes he is studying, he is personally interested in the results
of his reasoning, for he himself may be affected by it. If, as a
result of his analysis, he becomes convinced that the purpose
of government should be to achieve the greatest good of the
greatest number, and if he is also convinced that the surest
way to discover what that good is is to consult each individual
and to accept the majority view, as the nearest possible
approximation to the ideal, then he cannot logically feel
affronted if that majority decides that he has too many of the
goods of this world and others too few, and proceeds to redistribute them. If he and his ancestors have been property-
owners for generations, then it is unlikely that he will reach
this conclusion. It is no accident that property-owners are, as
a general rule, believers in the institution of private property.
They believe in it, not because they are clinging selfishly to
their possessions and ignoring the good of the community, but
because they have never been able to look at the problem from
outside. They have always seen it through the spectacles of
property-owners, and these lead them to see some things more
and others less clearly than those who are looking at them
through the spectacles of a propertyless class. Not all of us
would agree with Mr. Quintin Hogg's description of Conservatives. "The simplest among them", he says, "prefer fox-
hunting—the wisest religion."[1] His experience leads him to

---

[1] *The Case for Conservatism* (Penguin Books, 1947), p. 10.

see them in that light, just as the experience of a Communist worker may lead him to see them as capitalist exploiters of the poor.

It was one of Marx's great achievements that he saw, more clearly than had been seen before, the extent to which the economic conditions in which we are born and brought up determine our mental outlook. But our personal make-up is determined, too, by many other factors, religious, social or psychological, some due to heredity, others to environment. As students of politics, we can never detach ourselves from them to the extent to which the natural scientist can detach his personal preoccupations from the problems that he is studying. When Leslie Stephen wrote that "the philosopher has his passions like other men", when Laski wrote that "men think differently who live differently", both were emphasizing this limitation on the objectivity of the political thinker. He can never alter the fact that he comes to consider the problem of human relationships in society with a mind which is not open, which is not, to use Locke's phrase, a *tabula rasa*. His outlook has already been formed by his experience as a citizen of a country with a particular history, who looks at events from the angle of one sex, class or profession, rather than another. He will have obsessions, blind spots, personal preoccupations; he will highlight some facts and pass over others because some have made a stronger impact on his mind than others. Thomas Hobbes grew up in the years preceding the Civil Wars, when the power of absolute monarchy was challenged by parliamentarian and republican forces. He was obsessed by the problem of law and order, by the conviction that only a strong ruler could prevent society from degenerating into anarchy, into a battlefield in which man would destroy his fellows. Whether or not he was influenced by the actual disorders of the period of civil war, he was certainly influenced by a strong personal conviction that men were naturally evil and quarrelsome. He saw mankind through pessimistic spectacles, whereas his younger contemporary, Locke, was led, both by temperament and experience, to see his fellow men in a different light. Locke thought that men were naturally pleasant and peaceable and could be trusted to govern themselves. Because his experience brought him into contact with the practical problems of administration, he was concerned to work out the methods by which the different organs of government could best co-operate in safeguarding men from the dangers of abuse of power by their rulers. "This freedom from arbitrary power", he wrote, "is so necessary to and closely joined with a man's preservation that he cannot part with it but by what forfeits his preservation and life together."[1] Writing nearly a century later, Rousseau thought of government in terms of States small enough for the citizen to participate directly in the task. No doubt he was led to think of government in this way, both by his temperament and by his experience as a citizen of Geneva, which had, in fact, governed itself in this way. To-day, when industrial expansion has brought into existence vast urban agglomerations and greatly extended State functions, we think of government in terms of parties and Parliamentary representatives. Circumstances have changed and so have our habits of mind. Rousseau distrusted formal education, partly, no doubt, because he himself was ill-educated and suffered from what we should call to-day an inferiority complex. He was unconsciously biased, as a political philosopher, by his personal experience. Indeed, some writers have gone so far as to say that the clue to understanding Rousseau is always to be found in his own psychological history. "Each of Rousseau's attacks on the existing social system", says one writer, "each of the remedies he proposed for its transformation, sprang out of his own passionate misery and his consciousness of the miseries of others."[2]

Some of the most striking examples of the unconscious bias of the political thinker are provided by what is called national

---

[1] *Of Civil Government*, (Everyman Edition), §17.
[2] Kingsley Martin, *French Liberal Thought in the Eighteenth Century* (Benn, 1929), p. 195.

character. "The New Hebrides native, the Chinese peasant, and the American millionaire breathe in the same physical air, but a different social atmosphere. They have not made it or constructed it or thought it out: it has made them what they are, and their spiritual life is as impossible without it as physical life is without physical air. It has given to them, each in a different way, the scale of values, the religion, the interests which they possess; and though they may change it slightly or criticize it, they can no more think themselves out of it than they can think themselves out of breathing."[1] To quote one example, the differences in social atmosphere, or political heredity, of the French and British democracies certainly help to explain why the two countries have had such different attitudes to supra-national institutions. In the 1950's, the conception of a supra-national authority seemed to many Frenchmen to be a logical starting point, whereas it seemed to many Englishmen that it could come only as a culmination. The French point of view is that of a nation with a tradition of written constitutions, drawn up to define precisely the framework within which political institutions were expected to function, while the British habit of mind is one which likes to experiment in practice, before drawing up theoretical rules which are intended to be permanent. The British tend to take their pragmatism for granted, because they have enjoyed a long history of peaceful political evolution. Their security from foreign invasion has made political experiments less risky for them. French democracy has always felt itself to be threatened by enemies inside the State as well as outside. It has sought reassurance from legal and constitutional documents, precisely because it is not sure how firm its foundations are. The British, who are convinced, rightly or wrongly, that their own democratic foundations are safe, tend to regard legalistic definitions as more likely to tie their hands than to provide support. Or, to put it differently, they tend to think

---

[1] R. H. S. Crossman, *Government and the Governed* (Christopher, 1947), p. 3.

in terms of experiment and improvization in foreign affairs, because they have been able to rely on stable government at home. The French have sought to build "Europe" partly as a defence against insecurity inside as well as outside their frontiers, and both nations take for granted the "national" elements in their "international" policies.

If it is necessary not to underestimate the importance of these subjective elements in the make-up of political scientists, politicians and citizens, it is equally necessary not to exaggerate their importance. Natural scientists, too, can be subjective. Many are, no doubt, equally passionately interested in the results of their researches and some allow their interpretation of facts to be coloured by their desires, or by their particular approach or speciality. There are cases of illnesses which are difficult to diagnose, where a surgeon has been known to recommend an operation and a physician treatment, because the natural bias of each has supplemented inadequate data. There are vegetarian and carnivorous medical men, those who are biased in favour of, or against, psychological treatment. Specialists disagree in all sciences. But the personal bias of the scientist is bound to play a more important part in the ill-defined field of political science, where the facts are difficult to observe and impossible to isolate and where data are rarely adequate to justify provisional, let alone verifiable hypotheses. That should not lead us to make too much of the subjective elements and to try to explain political philosophies entirely in terms of psychological, economic or historical determinism. This is the "fashionable" approach to political science in the twentieth century—the century of Marxism and psycho-analysis—just as the rationalist approach was fashionable in the eighteenth century and the nationalist approach in the nineteenth. Rationalist Frenchmen in the eighteenth century underestimated personal and national differences and sought principles of universal validity. The early revolutionaries, still under the influence of the eighteenth-century philosophers, were convinced that they were on the way to

solving, not only France's political problems, but also those of
the world. France was merely showing the way. Boissy d'Anglas
explained how the revolutionaries looked at the Empire.
The colonies, he said, would all have the same forms of
administration as France. There was only one good way to
administer a country and if they had found it for Europe why
should other people not benefit by it? In 1793, Anacharsis
Clootz, one of the revolutionary constitution-makers, was in
favour of the establishment of a universal republic, of which
the following were to be the constitutional principles:—

1.   The only sovereign is the human race.
2.   Individuals or local communities accepting this
     luminous and immutable principle shall be members
     in their own right of our fraternal association, the
     universal Republic of men and brothers.
3.   Where there is no common frontier or maritime
     contact, local communities or distant enclaves shall
     await propagation of the truth before admission to
     membership.[1]

The human desire for certainty as to what constitutes the
"good life", or the best form of government, is very deep-
rooted and the current attitude, influenced as it is by the
discoveries of individual and social psychology, represents
merely one phase in the long history of assumptions about the
nature of man as a political and social animal. It is conditioned by the atmosphere of the twentieth century, just as the
rationalism and universalism of the *philosophes* and the
early revolutionaries was part of the atmosphere of the
eighteenth century, just as theories of national self-deter-
mination dominated much of the progressive thought of the
nineteenth century. Although we may not be able to "think
ourselves out" of our background, although we are inevitably
conditioned to a large extent by the general atmosphere

---

[1] Quoted in Duguit, Monnier and Bonnard, *Les Constitutions et les principales lois politiques de
la France*, p. 34 (1943 ed.).

of our time, as well as by the particular habits and traditions
of the environment which is familiar to us, we can, at least,
think *about* it, try to take it into account, try to distinguish
between opinions which we hold because we are convinced
that they are correct and those which we have taken over
unquestioningly from our parents, or our friends. For example,
the context in which the enquiries which we are making in
this book are carried out is that of the twentieth century, as
seen from the angle of a British citizen and a democrat who
first studied the problems of politics during the period between
the two world wars. This means that the writer—and probably
also the reader—will tend to take for granted certain assúmp-
tions about political organization which might be less readily
accepted elsewhere. Most British citizens to-day accept without question the normality of the democratic procedure to
which they are accustomed. They are conditioned, for example,
to accept as normal universal suffrage at the age of eighteen,
instead of, as formerly, at twenty-one. They accept compulsory education between the ages of five and sixteen, and
retirement between sixty and sixty-five. Some countries have
made different choices and have had different attitudes to
the enfranchisement of women and coloured people. Britain
does not feel that those entitled to vote should be compelled
to do so or to satisfy tests of educational ability. On every
political problem we shall discover divergencies between the
attitudes of people with different social and political traditions.
Sometimes they will be national divergencies, sometimes
class differences, sometimes personal differences of interpretation regarding the implications of this or that policy
theory.

The study of politics, then, is not likely to lead us to any
final conclusions about what is the "right" or "best" form of
political organization. It would be unrealistic to argue, however, that, since certainty on anything seems impossible of
attainment, we might as well contract out of the whole business
and leave the study of politics to those who are interested in,

or have time for, speculations that do not seem to lead anywhere. Very few of the activities in which the human race
finds pleasure lead anywhere. Cricket, football pools, cross-
word puzzles, detective stories are all subjects of study as
well as forms of amusement. To some people, the study of
politics is more fascinating still and needs no further justification. But for those who need to be convinced that political
speculation serves some practical purpose, there is another
answer. In a democracy, as the British understand it, every
individual counts for one, the thoughtless rank equally with the
thoughtful, the non-voter counts for as much as the voter. All
that the citizen achieves by deciding to take no interest in
politics is to hand over the control of affairs, and of affairs
which concern him vitally, to others, to deny himself the
amount of say in the matter which the constitution accords
him. By deciding that he does not count, he automatically
allows those who do participate in politics to count for more
than one and, to that extent, to decide his future for him.

Nor need the citizen be unduly deterred from the study of
politics by the fact that its subject-matter is less precise than
that of the natural sciences. If the political scientist cannot
reach conclusions which can be regarded as "laws", in the
sense in which we speak of the law of gravity, if he is neither
a doctor nor a prophet, he can, nevertheless, play a valuable
part in helping the citizen to make up his mind on political
matters. His rôle is rather like that of the constitutional
monarch as defined by Bagehot in the middle of the last
century. His function is "to encourage and to warn".[1] He
is guide, philosopher and friend and, if need be, Cassan-
dra. He can show us "how the wheels go round", how and
why this or that policy may be dangerous. We can learn from
the achievements and mistakes of past and present generations,
and from the politics of other countries, we can learn what are
the issues which, rightly or wrongly, men have cared most

---

[1] *The English Constitution* (Worlds Classics, 1928), p. 67.

about, what they have died for, or sacrificed their liberty for, what degree of injustice or frustration they have found intolerable.

It is likely that the study of these questions will, at least, sharpen our wits and help us to see below the surface of things. It may even help us to find more satisfactory solutions for some of our present political problems, even if it brings us no nearer to finding an answer to the fundamental problems of political organization. Like the medical student who cannot create life artificially, or say of what it consists, we cannot say with any certainty whether the ultimate purpose of politics should be to achieve happiness, liberty or equality. We can only form our own tentative conclusions on the basis of the evidence provided by our study of politics. But we can learn to understand better a number of problems which have a more immediate impact on our lives. We can learn how to lessen some forms of suffering, such as those that result from poverty and unemployment. We can help to create well-being. We can learn to explain more intelligibly to others why we support one method of achieving certain ends and reject another. In other words, what the study of politics can do for us is to help us to know our own minds more clearly, to choose this rather than that form of political activity from conscious principle, rather than from unthinking habit. It will not necessarily change our political convictions. But at least it will help us to know *why* we are Conservatives, Liberals, Socialists or Communists.

This explanation of why we ought, as citizens, to be interested in politics would not be accepted as adequate by everyone. Some thinkers would claim for the science of politics a much higher degree of precision. In the context of the opinions expressed above, it is not important whether or not we call the conclusions which we reach "scientific". For some thinkers, however, politics is, or can be, not an art—"the art of the possible" as a Frenchman once defined it—but a science which can become as exact as applied economics. One writer

goes so far as to define politics as "a science of predictions".[1]
Politics, he goes on, "is a science in that it consists of a body
of verifiable and systematic knowledge, gathered by observation and experiment." He holds that the predictions which
the political scientist makes as the result of his observation
and experiment are sufficiently accurate to rank as scientific
laws, and he quotes as an example the conclusion regarding
the influence of power which has been mentioned earlier in
this chapter. "That every body of men in power will tend to
acquire to themselves more power, is not," he says, "a statement which need fear serious challenge." Such statements, or
observations, regarding "consistencies of conduct, . . . recurring
age after age, although varying contextually with the particular conditions (for history never identically repeats itself)" are,
he goes on, sufficiently formal "for it to be possible tentatively
to put forward hypotheses as to concomitant or consequent
lines of conduct, which hypotheses, upon constant reverifica-
tion, can be accounted laws."

This approach seems either to claim too much for politics,
or to make its laws so general and so hedged about with
qualifications or "reverifications" as to be useless for any
practical purposes. It is difficult to imagine any political
"law" whose application would be as simple and straight-
forward as, say, the law of gravity. If you release your grip
on an apple, it will fall to the ground. If you release it in a
vacuum it will fall with an acceleration of thirty-two feet
per second per second. Such a statement belongs to a
totally different category from a "law" which proclaims,
in Lord Acton's words, that "power tends to corrupt, and
absolute power corrupts absolutely". The statement may be
unchallengeable. But, as it stands, it gives us no guidance
which will enable us to recognize the point at which power is
in danger of abuse. Some power is necessary, or society, in
the absence of government, will lapse into anarchy or chaos.

[1] Catlin, *The Science and Method of Politics* (Kegan Paul, 1926).

Therefore too little power, as well as too much, is bad. By what signs can we measure the point at which there is neither too little nor too much, but enough, and by what methods can we ensure that the desired equilibrium will be reached and maintained? These are the real problems of politics, and, however true the general laws, or predictions, of political science may be, they are of little use if they do not help us to find answers to these questions. We can make a great many observations about what men have done in certain defined circumstances. We can explain these actions as bearing witness to the truth of some political "law" or "prediction". But until the events have happened, and even after, our reasoning is always open to challenge.

It seems, therefore, more realistic to assume that there exists no systematic body of knowledge that can, to use MacIver's phrase, "serve as a definite guide to the Statesman, a science of how to govern, an applied science that does or can do in its field what medicine, say, or engineering does in its field". "Political science", said Harold Laski, "has not the axiomatic quality of mathematics. In its equations the variables are human beings whose uniqueness prevents their reduction to law in the scientific sense of that much-abused word."

Whether or not we believe politics to be a science in the sense in which the above writers define it, we can agree on at least three ways in which the study of politics can help us to order our lives better. First, as has been said, by drawing attention to the pattern of history, to the danger signals, historians and political scientists can help us to learn from history. When South Korea was invaded in June, 1950, politicians and political commentators urged us not to make the mistake that we made in 1938. They were not drawing exact parallels, nor claiming any infallibility in their predictions. They were pointing out the existence of certain facts which seemed to them to warrant the assumption that a familiar pattern might be repeated, and warning us of the consequences which we might expect if their analysis were to prove correct? "We deal with tendencies," said Harold Laski, "we can predict upon the basis of experience. But our predictions are limited by the necessity of recognizing that the facts are not within our control. We can influence and attempt and hope; the certainty and precision of the chemist, or even the physiologist, can never be ours."

The second contribution which the study of politics can make to the art or science of government is to add to our knowledge of the political forces which go to make up national and group attitudes. We may come no nearer to agreeing with, say, South African attitudes to coloured people, the sectarian violence of Northern Ireland, or Swiss neutrality, but we can come nearer to understanding how they came to be adopted and why they persist. Explanations of why people held certain views in the past often throw light on the reasons why others hold similar views to-day, because we are not merely products of our past, but very largely prisoners of it. Many of the ideas to which we cling turn out, on examination, to be irrational prejudices, whose persistence is due to habit, not reason. When we begin to ask *why* we do certain things or think in certain ways, we often have to look back into history to find the answers, and we sometimes find, not only that we can discover no valid reason for our attitude, but also that other countries or other people have found different and more satisfactory answers. To quote one or two simple examples, why do the British and Americans express their political opinions, in the main, through the medium of two large parties, whereas other countries have multi-party systems? Why are the lines of cleavage between the two American and the two British parties so different? Why is the American Socialist Party so small and the French Communist Party so large? When we can answer these and other questions, we shall not only come nearer to understanding the problems of our neighbours, we shall probably understand our own problems better as well.

Lastly, the study of politics, even if it does not make the average citizen feel less helpless in face of the national and international problems of his time, does at least help him to know more accurately what he himself feels about them. He can discover what *he* really means when he uses terms like "Fascist", "Red", "democracy", "tyranny", "inequality", even if he is not always sure what his neighbour means by them. He can learn how much or how little political action can reasonably be expected to achieve, and how fast or how slow the advance is likely to be in given conditions. He can learn not to count on miracles or to base his hopes on wild miscalculations of the potentialities of human behaviour. In other words, he can learn to be an intelligent and balanced citizen.

CHAPTER TWO

The Problem of Power in the State

THE study of politics, says Laski, "concerns itself with the life of men in relation to organized States". It is necessary, therefore, to be clear, right at the outset, what we mean by "States". "The State" is a term freely used in current political propaganda. We hear a great deal about "the Welfare State", "State control", "State bureaucracy". In general election campaigns, we usually find that "the State" comes in for a good deal of criticism by Conservatives, and often by Liberals, who object to State monopolies, or to what they regard as excessive State restriction of individual freedom. Socialist parties, on the other hand, tend to regard the State as a real or potential creator of individual well-being. They praise the achievements of the welfare state, and approve the principle of State-run industries, sometimes advocating extension of the public sector.

In practice, decisions to give the State a large or a small part in political life, or to increase or restrict its functions, are always executed by Governments. Does this mean that when we speak of the State, we mean simply the Government? In everyday language the two words are often used as if they were interchangeable. In reality, however, they are not synonymous, for it is perfectly possible to conceive of communities—primitive, nomadic tribes, for example—which are not "States" in the sense in which Great Britain and the United States of America are States, but which have government in the sense of accepted rules of conduct, by which law and order are maintained. Indeed, it could be argued, says MacIver, that "where the family exists—and it exists everywhere in human society—

government already exists." If this is so, government can exist independently of national States.

Is the clue, then, to the meaning of the term "the State" the fact that it is national? Certainly, the modern State is limited by national frontiers. We are members of the State within whose frontiers we are born and we can change our State allegiance or nationality only with the permission of the State to which we want to belong. Yet the State is no more synonymous with the nation than with the Government. The Scots and the Welsh have for long seen themselves as nations but have only recently sought in serious numbers to become wholly or partially separate States. At times, States have annexed nations. Alsace and Lorraine were from 1870 to 1914 part of the German State and their citizens elected members to the German Reichstag. From 1918 to 1940, they formed part of France and elected Deputies to the French Parliament. From 1940 to 1945, they formed part of the Westmark of Hitler's Reich. To-day, they are once more part of France. If you ask an Alsatian whether he is French or German, he will certainly reply that he is Alsatian and he may add that he is also French. In the 'thirties, some Alsatians would have argued that they ought to be independent of both France and Germany, in other words, that they *ought* to form an Alsatian "State".

The concept of a nation is not easy to define with precision. It includes people of the same race and who speak the same language, but by no means exclusively. The United States and four former British Dominions recognize English as their mother tongue (although two of them also have other languages) and all have racial links with England, but they are distinct and separate nations and also independent States. Switzerland, on the other hand, is a nation in which there are three races, four official languages and a number of local dialects which are far more generally spoken than the official languages. The Swiss, who are united by neither racial nor linguistic bonds, are as patriotic and as conscious of their common membership of a nation as any other people. Both France and Spain have a Basque population, speaking a language of unknown origin and not spoken anywhere else in the world, but the Basques do not form a nation any more than do Welsh and Breton Celts. Yet in both cases, there is a common racial and linguistic inheritance. The Sudeten Germans, who were members of the Czech State, felt themselves in the 'thirties to be Germans. Most Cypriots feel themselves to be Turkish Cypriots or Greek Cypriots, not simply Cypriots. The Jews provide the most striking example of the distinction between national consciousness and Statehood. British, French and Israeli Jews, for example, are all conscious of a common racial bond and they may or may not have a common linguistic bond. Yet all three belong to different States and use different languages in their everyday life and they may feel more conscious of the national loyalties that separate them than of the bonds that unite them. A Zionist and a non-Zionist have equal status as members of the State of which they are citizens, but the former feels a stronger sense of loyalty than the latter to the State of Israel, although he may not seek to become an Israeli citizen.

A sense of national unity, of nationalism is, then, no necessary guarantee of nationality—that is, of membership of a nation State. Indeed, one difficulty in regarding the State as being merely another name for the nation is the fact that the State, acting through the Government, has the power to determine an individual's nationality. A Stateless person may be a native of Lithuania or Poland or some other country, in the sense that he was born there, and may feel that he belongs to the one country whose language is his mother-tongue. But he can be a citizen of that country only if the State agrees. In 1948, an American called Garry Davis, who had renounced his American citizenship, established himself in Paris, where the United Nations Assembly was in session, calling himself a citizen of the world. He found that "the world" could not provide him with a passport. Having no national status, he had no possibility of leading a normal life and was eventually compelled to go back to the United States and ask to be regranted American citizenship.

The State, then, is something distinct from both nation and Government, though its nature cannot be understood without reference to both. For a State is limited by national frontiers and every act which we recognize as an act of the State is in the end an act by a Government. A Government may be set up in different ways; it may be chosen by the people, or imposed on them by force, but in either case, it acts as the recognized agent of the State. "When we speak of the State", says MacIver, "we mean the organization of which Government is the administrative organ. . . . A State has a constitution, a code of laws, a way of setting up its government, a body of citizens. When we think of this whole structure we think of the State."

This may be true, but other national organizations besides the State have a constitution, a code of laws and a way of setting up their governments; churches, political parties, Trade Unions, for example. What is it that differentiates the State from any other association?

First, there is the element of compulsion which enters into the relationship between the citizen and the State. The citizen cannot choose whether he will be a member of a particular State, as he can choose whether to join a Church or a Trade Union. Second, there is the fact that all other organizations and activities within the national frontiers are, in the last resort, subordinate to the State. The power of the State, or, as we see it in action, the power of the Government, is formally supreme, in the sense that the conditions in which we are born, grow up, are educated, work, enjoy our leisure, own property, marry, have children and die are all laid down by the State, and the Government can compel us to comply with them. All births must be registered; otherwise all kinds of complications can arise. There was an actual case in France where a man, one of twins, discovered, when he wanted to get

married, that only his twin's birth had been registered. He
discovered, too, that his parents' omission meant that, as far
as the State was concerned, he did not exist. He was virtually
unable to take a step until he had gone through the complicated legal formalities which repairing his parents' omission
entailed. Similarly, parents are obliged to send their children
to school for a certain number of years or to satisfy the
authorities that they are making adequate provisions for their
education in some other way. They are obliged to notify the
authorities if they suffer from certain infectious diseases. If
you have a disease such as typhoid fever, or smallpox, the
State Health authorities will proceed to trace the people with
whom you have been in contact, or the retailer from whom you
buy your milk, and advise, or in come cases compel, them to
take certain courses of action. Citizens must pay taxes to the
State, whether they approve of the uses to which the money
is put or not. They must maintain their houses in reasonable
repair, keep them reasonably clean, clothe themselves decently,
behave with propriety in the street, avoid making themselves
a nuisance to their neighbours, and they must respect the
persons and property of other people. In monogamous States
they may have only one wife (or husband) at a time and may
marry her only at certain prescribed hours of the day and in
certain prescribed places, in accordance with certain prescribed
procedures. They must maintain their wives and the children
of their marriages, they may obtain a divorce only for certain
specific reasons, must comply with certain formalities when
their wives die and must bury them only in certain places.
As workers or employers, citizens are obliged to obey a number
of rules, as laid down in the Factory Acts, for example, or the
Catering Wages Act. Any citizen who fails to comply with
any regulation, even if it is so small a thing as observing
lighting-up time, is liable to find himself brought before a
court of law, where his case will be heard, again in accordance
with a procedure which the State lays down, and, if found
guilty, he will be punished in a way which the State decides is

suitable. Even in his leisure hours the citizen cannot escape the State's control. If he joins a political party, he will not be allowed to preach what the State defines as "sedition". He may not lead a band of followers into the House of Commons, shouting "We want a Republic". If an election is announced, he will not, if he is a candidate, be allowed to buy an elector in his constituency a glass of beer. If he joins a church, he may not claim exemption from secular laws on the ground of his religion; he may not, for example, argue that since a Moslem is allowed more than one wife, he may, if he belongs to that faith, commit bigamy with impunity. If he wants to place a bet on a horse, he must do so only in the way provided for by legislation. If he wants to drink a glass of beer or buy a packet of cigarettes, he may do so only at certain hours of the day. If he gives a party in his own house, he may find himself summoned by a neighbour for making too much noise, in which case he will have to appear in Court, and may be punished by the State.

There is, in fact, hardly a single human activity which is not in some way regulated by the State. The State is, thus, the sovereign power in a nation. It is, in the words of a French writer of the sixteenth century, a body which gives orders to all and receives orders from none. "The modern State", says Laski, "is a territorial society, divided into Government and subjects, claiming, within its allotted physical area, a supremacy over all other institutions." Or, as another definition puts it, it is "the institution, or group of institutions, which is entrusted with the government of a community known as a nation."[1]

We have said that what differentiates membership of the State from that of other associations is its compulsory nature and the fact that the State lays down the framework within which all other exercises of power must function. This power to direct is a twofold power. The State gives the directions

---

[1] Jenks, *The Ship of State* (Duckworth, 1949), p. 11.

and it also enforces them, if necessary by employing armed force. The State is the only association within the national frontiers which can use the nation's armed forces to compel obedience to its orders. How essential that control is to the State's effective power is one of the clearest lessons of history. The Government's failure to control the army helps to explain the weakness in the 'thirties of the Weimar and Spanish Republics, and the fall of the Fourth French Republic in 1958. Lenin recognized the importance of the army when he included control of it among the essential conditions of a successful revolution. The British Parliament recognized it in the seventeenth century when it sought to restrict the right of the monarch to maintain a standing army. "The basis of state-sovereignty," said Laski, "is the contingent power to use the armed forces of the state to compel obedience to its will. . . . And it is the possession of this legal right to resort to coercion which distinguishes the government of the state from the government of all other associations."

This definition of the State in terms of power may be formally satisfactory, in that it explains where power resides while it is unchallenged. It explains the nature of the relationship between Government and governed as long as the latter do in actual fact approve of, or acquiesce in, the decisions of the former. It does not tell us what causes subjects to decide at times to cease to accept the rule of one Government and to replace it by another. Governments change, sometimes peacefully, sometimes as a result of revolution. When that happens, the new Government is supreme, as was its predecessor, but something of importance to the citizens has happened. The power of the new Government may be used for quite different ends from those which the previous Government pursued. A definition in terms of power is unsatisfactory in that it does not tell us anything about those ends.

All Governments may be alike in being formally supreme, but, in actual practice, Governments vary widely in the way they use their power. An absolute monarch is not bound to take any account of the wishes of his subjects. When Louis XIV said "I am the State," what he really meant was: "I am the Government and what I say goes". In a dictatorship, too, the Government is not responsible to the nation for the way in which it uses its power, though it usually retains some of the democratic vocabulary and the formal framework of democratic institutions. Louis XIV did not have a Parliament; Hitler retained the Reichstag as a subservient organ whose function was merely to record formal approval of Nazi policy. In a parliamentary democracy, the nation itself, through the medium of its electorate and its Parliament, decides in greater or less detail the way in which a Government shall use its power. Both Government and people agree to bind themselves, the one to act in accordance with the wishes of the electorate and to accept the latter's verdict on its performance, the other to change a Government which does not meet with its approval only in accordance with a procedure laid down in advance. The form of the agreement varies. There may be a written constitution, or written laws, supplemented to a greater or less extent by unwritten laws, conventions, traditions and customs. But the principle remains the same. The last word remains with the people. Indeed, in some democratic States there often seems to be, says Laski, "a larger degree of obedience from the sovereign Parliament to its constituents than there is the other way round; a series of by-elections, for instance, produce with amazing rapidity a change in the will and temper of the sovereign."

The fact that, in a democracy, the Government is bound by its responsibility to the nation to use its power only in certain ways approved by the people has led some thinkers to challenge the definition of the State in terms of sovereign power, exercised on its behalf by the Government. If the nation has the last word, then, they argue, the nation is in reality sovereign. Yet, each citizen of the nation is individually bound to obey his Government. If he tries to resist, he will find himself in a position similar to that of the man who tried to visit a defence area without a permit, on the ground that he was one of the owners.

The nineteenth-century constitutional lawyer, Dicey, tried to escape from the dilemma by making a distinction between legal and political sovereignty.[1] In Britain, he said, while Parliament was 'from a legal point of view' the sovereign legislative power in the State, it was, from a political point of view, subject to two practical limitations. It could not enforce its will if the governed refused to obey and, since it was itself made up of individuals whose outlook was formed by the same social climate as that of their constituents, there were things that it would not, in practice, dream of trying to do, however extensive its legal competence might be. "If a legislature decided that all blue-eyed babies should be murdered," said Leslie Stephen, "the preservation of blue-eyed babies would be illegal, but legislators must go mad before they could pass such a law and subjects be idiotic before they could submit to it."[2]

This distinction between the legal and the political aspects of sovereignty is useful, in that it reminds us that we are dealing with the power, not of an inanimate machine, but of human beings over their fellow-men. It is not possible to define in quantitative terms how much exercise of power by the State the citizen will stand without revolting, because the amount will vary with historical, geographical and ideological conditions. But we know from history that, however absolute the legal right to exercise power may be, there is a limit in practice. Human beings will stand just so much. Among the real but intangible factors which help a Government to know when it is in danger of overstepping the mark are the common social traditions which, as Dicey said, have formed the outlook of both Government and governed. There are certain things which, quite literally, cannot be done at a particular time and in a particular place. The above example

---

[1] *The Law of the Constitution*, 1915, Introduction, pp xviii-xix.
[2] *Science of Ethics*, p. 143.

is pertinent, if extreme. But how long would a British Government or Parliament last, which tried to abolish church-going or women's suffrage, or to establish State-controlled Trade Unions, compulsory voting or a single political party? Yet these objectives have all been pursued, at one time or another, in one country or another.

It is this incalculable reserve of power possessed by the governed which makes it difficult to decide where, in a State, ultimate power really resides. At any moment of time, immediate power belongs to the Government, which alone can enforce obedience to its will. If we look at a nation over a longer period of time, we see that, in parliamentary systems at least, the representative legislature is the source of the Government's power, since it alone can determine the content of the laws to which the Government can compel obedience. In the long run, however, a Parliament which legislates in a manner contrary to the will of the people will be replaced by one more faithful to the popular will. The Belgian constitution resolved the problem in the following formula: "All powers emanate from the nation; they are exercised in the manner established by the Constitution." The French constitution of 1946, and that of 1958, both use similar formulæ.

The doctrine of popular sovereignty, which attributes ultimate power to the nation, that is, to the citizens acting either directly, as in certain Swiss Cantons, or indirectly through their legally accredited representatives, as democracies act to-day, is a concept which at first sight seems theoretically satisfactory. Yet it leaves a number of practical problems unresolved. It assumes, first, not only that there is such a thing as the will of a society, but also that society can express its will. When "the people" are called on to decide something, what guarantee is there that they can ever agree and, if they do not, how can we speak of national "representatives"? Modern States have adopted the indirect system of government, by means of elected representatives, because a

country with millions of inhabitants knows of no other practicable method of popular consultation. It assumes, without
any proof, that accurate representation is possible and,
further, that it is actually achieved. Now, it is possible to argue
that votes cast for this or that candidate or party can represent what the elector wants on balance, but only in so far as
it is possible for him to choose between a simple "Yes" and
"No". Most of us would prefer to accept some and reject other
items of a candidate's programme, but we realize that, if
allowance had to be made for individual or group shades of
opinion, the whole system of popular election would be
rendered so unwieldy that it would be bound to break down.
We accept compromises, in order to make a clear and positive
electoral verdict possible. If we look at the process for a
moment, not as practical voters, but as students of politics,
we are bound to ask ourselves whether the millions of individual compromises represented by ballot papers can be said
to add up to anything that could justifiably be described as
the will of the people. If we were all equally intelligent and
equally articulate, then it might be claimed that the result was
as close an approximation to the will of the people as was
humanly possible in the circumstances. But do all views
count equally? Some of us understand the questions at issue
better than others; some of us are better able to persuade
others to adopt our point of view. If we ask ourselves what
makes the average elector vote one way or another, we are
bound to conclude that the influences of history and social
tradition are supplemented by the direct or indirect pressure
of a host of other influences; of family, friends, the Church,
the Press, for example. Some of these influences are much more
vocal than others. If I want to plead for support for some
policy, I can reach, at most, a few hundred ears. The editor
of a national daily paper can speak to millions of electors.

   Where, in all this complexity and confusion, is the voice of
the people? Whose opinions are really represented, behind the
façade of universal suffrage? Some thinkers have answered

these questions by rejecting the whole concept of sovereignty, popular or other, as an unhelpful abstraction. The real rulers of a society, it has been said, are undiscoverable. Others have tried to sort out the dominant forces in a State, to which real leadership belongs. Marx concluded that, in nineteenth century capitalist society, the holders of economic power were able to dominate the political machine. The State was nothing more than the agent of the ruling classes. The only way, therefore, to reach a position where men could have an equal chance of making their voices heard was to get rid of the exploitation of one class by another and to create a classless society, where there was real equality between man and man. When that happened, the State, as an instrument of class domination, would wither away and government would consist of the administration of publicly owned wealth by the whole society, in the interests of all.

The argument that political equality, unaccompanied by equality of economic opportunity, can be a sham was new and revolutionary when Marx wrote. Nowadays, however, many thinkers who recognize that there is much truth in the Marxian analysis argue that it over-simplifies the problem. "We cannot simplify the issue," writes MacIver, "and claim with the Marxists that economic power is always primary in capitalistic society and that political power is both its offspring and its servant. For in the first place economic power is multi-centred and is the scene of internecine warfare, business against business, industry against industry, capital against labour, industry seeking to cheapen agriculture and *vice versa*. ... ." Then again, "the relative ease with which powerful economic interests have been defeated in the political arena, the many encroachments of Governments, by taxation and regulation, on the prerogative of wealth, the progress of 'social legislation' all along the line, and the manner in which various Governments, without any proletarian revolution, have taken over such important sectors of capitalistic enterprise as railroads and public utilities demonstrate the inadequacy of the Marxian thesis to comprehend the complex relationship between economic and political power."

Other thinkers have held that leadership should belong to no one dominant section of the community, whether political or economic. "In a free Government," wrote one of the early American Republicans, "the security for civil rights must be the same as that for religious rights. It consists in the one case in the multiplicity of interests, and in the other in the multiplicity of sects. The degree of security in both cases will depend on the number of interests and sects."[1] Some political thinkers have argued that there ought to be constitutional safeguards against the possibility of domination by any *one* organ of Government, however constituted. In the United States Constitution, for example, power is shared between the Senate, representing the different States of the Union, the House of Representatives, democratically elected by popular suffrage, the President, chosen by the whole nation, and the Supreme Court, whose nine members are nominated for life. The eighteenth-century writer, Montesquieu, was a firm believer in this theory of "checks and balances", that is, of a division of power, not between different social and economic interests, but between different organs of government, so that no one organ could claim a degree of power that might degenerate into tyranny. With the advent of full Parliamentary democracy the sense of a need for such checks and balances has gone. The American is a significant exception among modern democratic constitutions.

The existence of rival pressures, whether political or economic, seems an inescapable fact in modern society, with the result that the concept of sovereignty seems on close examination to disintegrate. Laski argues, indeed, that "politically there is no such thing as sovereignty at all". There has never, he says, been a State "in which an actual identity of interest between rulers and subjects can be admitted". There are only

---

[1] Hamilton, *The Federalist* (Everyman Edition), LI, p. 266.

"different wills, some of which, from their strength, have more importance than others." "The State is only one of the associations to which he (i.e. the individual) happens to belong."

The citizen himself may, indeed, in his everyday life, be far more conscious of his membership of other associations than of his relationship to the State. "You do not state the total nature of Jones," says Laski, "by saying that he is a Wesleyan barrister who belongs to the Reform Club and the Ancient Order of Oddfellows." But Jones may well *feel* that his total nature is expressed in these activities and go through life, oblivious of the extent to which, in reality, the State regulates his life from birth to death. Even if he is passionately interested in politics, he is still not a "political animal" all the time. He is conscious of a number of other loyalties, some of which may take priority over his loyalty to the State. Members of the Society of Friends have a conscientious objection to being conscripted into the army, because they consider it morally wrong to fight for one's country. Christian Scientists are liable to come into conflict with the State because they do not believe in orthodox medical treatment of illness. Some suffragettes deliberately infringed the law as a protest against the State's refusal to grant them the right to vote. There have been times when Protestants were persecuted in France and Catholics penalized in Great Britain. There are Communists whose loyalty to their party is stronger than their loyalty to their country.

In cases like these, the State is formally supreme in that the Government can either enforce obedience or get rid of the offender, if necessary by condemning him to death. But the "assent" which the State can secure is one of outward conformity only. Much can be done to induce assent by pressure and persecution. Thus, Hitler imprisoned and tortured thousands of democrats, but he did not stamp them out, any more than Louis XIV stamped out French Protestants. A State can suppress beliefs, only in the sense that it can prohibit public profession of them. Future generations may invent monstrous television screens on which thoughts are recorded, like that imagined by George Orwell in his "1984". Up to now, however, the State has no machinery for controlling thoughts, or at least none that goes as far as this.

Men's views on the extent to which the State is justified in interfering with the pattern of the individual's life as he wants to live it have varied widely at different periods of history and from one country to another. In the Europe of the Middle Ages, individual freedom as we understand it to-day was as yet an unfamiliar concept. Life was ruled by tradition and custom, whose control was no less rigid than that of the most demanding State. Church and State ruled together, the one in the moral, the other in the temporal sphere. The duties of the temporal power were to maintain law and order, to dispense justice and to conduct dealings with foreign States. While there were no good roads and the only method of transport was the horse, the average individual lived in a small and isolated community, in which he was far more conscious of the impact on his life of his employer, the lord of the manor and the priest, than he was of the State.

With the growth of industry and commerce in the sixteenth and seventeenth centuries, the rigid mediæval system of control, based on custom and tradition, gave way to more flexible systems of private enterprise. These were encouraged by Governments, which saw in increased production and exchange the means of increasing national resources and so of increasing national power and prestige. But while men were set free from one set of controls, another kind was coming into being. For example, with the Reformation, the State became head of the Church in England and the duty of looking after the poor, which had been largely a moral obligation, devolved upon the State which had encouraged the replacement of the mediæval feudal relationship by that of employer-worker and which had dissolved the monasteries and religious orders. From the beginning of the seventeenth century, the relief of destitution became an obligation imposed by the State on all local com-

munities. In France, the rhythm of change was different and
feudal relationships persisted right up to the revolution of
1789. In Russia, a rural, largely pre-industrial civilization
persisted right up to the revolution of 1917. In Britain, the
process of transformation to modern industrial capitalism in
the nineteenth century so changed the nature of her civilization
that radical changes in the relationship between the State and
the individual followed inevitably. The disastrous consequences
of industrial labour on the health of the new industrial
populations aroused enlightened public opinion and a whole
new series of regulations came into force, limiting the freedom
of all sections of the population. Employers and workers were
bound to respect certain labour conditions and the citizens as
a whole were bound to take certain precautions against the
spread of disease.

Nevertheless, in the England of the nineteenth century,
politicians and economists believed that the power of the
State should be used to interfere with individual relationships,
only in so far as intervention was necessary to prevent flagrant
abuses of humanitarian principles and to safeguard public
health. The modern concept of a welfare State, with the duty
of protecting the individual against natural inequalities and
misfortunes, was still unborn. The State was regarded rather
as a kind of umpire, standing at the ringside watching the
forces of competition creating a society divided into rich and
poor. Most people felt that it was natural and inevitable for
some to be rich and privileged and others to be poor and
miserable and that the State ought not to interfere with this
natural state of affairs, except to ensure conformity with some
rudimentary rules of the game. In 1801, Hannah More, who
devoted her life to helping the poor, wrote to some women
who had been suffering from famine and who had been
helped by the local gentry, explaining that the gentry would
not have been able to afford "such large supplies to the dis-
tresses of the poor, had they not denied themselves . . . many
indulgences to which their fortune at other times entitles

them." She hoped that the poor had accepted what had been done for them "as a matter of favour, not of right."[1]

The picture of society when Marx published the first volume of *Capital* in 1867 was not fundamentally different. He concluded that the State was using its power exclusively in the interests of the economically dominant class, and went on to propose revolution as the remedy. There were social reformers in the nineteenth century, however, who saw the State as the potential instrument by which a more just society could be created, without the upheaval of a revolution. It was the duty of the State, in their view, to interfere in what had been hitherto the citizen's private affairs, with the aim of increasing freedom from want and the frustration of poverty and disease and so of enabling the poor to compete on less unequal terms with their more privileged fellow citizens. With the social legislation of the nineteenth century, there was born a concept of positive State interference which was to develop during the following century into the social service State, with its comprehensive system of social security from the cradle to the grave.

At any given time, the prevailing view on what ought to be the State's sphere of action has largely determined the degree of freedom accorded to different groups and associations within the State. Thus, in Russia, where the State intervenes in every sphere of individual activity, conflict between the State and individuals or groups was for long considered unthinkable. If the genetic theories of a Lysenko were decreed to be "correct" and "bourgeois" music or art "degenerate", then scientists, artists and musicians, like other Soviet citizens, had to accept the verdict. In France, however, there has been, ever since the Revolution, a strong tradition of individual freedom of opinion. There were even a few Frenchmen who argued, in 1944, that the right of artists to express themselves freely could logically be held to include the right to betray

---

[1] Hammond, *The Town Labourer*, cit. Woolf, *After the Deluge*, p. 157.

their country, without thereby incurring the usual penalty suffered by traitors.

On thousands of issues, Governments have drawn the line in different places between the extremes of repression of individual liberty and toleration of its abuse. On the censorship of art, for example, the safeguarding of public morality or the family, on freedom of religious beliefs, the right to form Trade Unions, countries with differing histories, traditions and habits of government have come to different conclusions. What the State fears as a potential threat and what the citizen feels to be a reasonable degree of freedom from interference by the State are both subjective concepts, determined in the light of political convictions and the impact of events, that is, in the light of the prejudices, fears and beliefs which go to make up the social climate of the time and of the nation.

In practice, the difficulties encountered by groups within the State have always been a function of their potential conflict with the authority of the State. Churches, political associations and Trade Unions have been particularly suspect because they are powerful rival centres of attraction. Men will die for their faith or for what they believe to be justice, more readily sometimes than they will die for their country. In times of war, or of threatened civil war, States fear the growth of forces which may weaken national unity more than they do in conditions of internal and external security. The Catholic Church seemed a danger to the British Protestant State when the Reformation was less than a century away. In the twentieth century, it no longer does. In seventeenth-century France, the Catholic State persecuted Huguenots. In eighteenth-century England, the Anglican State resented the spread of Nonconformity. France remained an absolute monarchy up to 1789 and democratic and parliamentary government was not firmly established for more than a century after the revolution. Groups within the State have, therefore, always been regarded with suspicion, as potential threats to the stability of the State. The Catholic Church in particular, as the ally and partner of absolute monarchy, was distrusted by the revolutionaries and has continued to be distrusted by the mass of those whose political ideals are inspired by the principles of 1789. Progressive parties are opposed to an established Church and were, until recently, opposed to State support for Catholic schools. Anti-clerical Frenchmen regarded the degree of subsidization of Catholic schools provided for under the British Education Act of 1944 as carrying toleration to quixotic lengths.

This difference of outlook is almost wholly explicable in terms of the different political evolution of the two countries. France has always been a strongly centralized State, no less one and indivisible under a republican than under a monarchic form of government. Fear of diversity as a threat to national unity has been a natural concomitant of threats from within or without which have persisted throughout French history. Great Britain, secure from invasion throughout her history, was able to establish the principle of parliamentary government as early as the seventeenth century, and her political institutions have always been based on strong traditions of local independence. From the end of the seventeenth century, religious toleration was felt to be possible without endangering the security of the State. The last vestige of discrimination against Catholics, the refusal of their right to enter Parliament, vanished in 1829. To-day, there are Catholics in all political parties, no more on one side than on the other. But in France, the Catholic Church did not accept the Republic until almost the end of the nineteenth century and, right up to the war of 1939, Conservative and even anti-Republican parties contained a higher proportion of Catholics than did the others. It was not until 1959 that anti-clericalism seemed at long last to be ceasing to be a major factor in French political divisions.

In both France and Britain, Trade Unions had a long and hard struggle to establish their right to freedom of action in the industrial field. The whole idea of combination in order to obtain better conditions seemed wrong to the rulers of the early nineteenth century. In England, Trade Unions were prohibited as a criminal conspiracy and it was not until 1906, after a long struggle, much suffering and even persecution—as in the case of the Tolpuddle martyrs in 1834—that their right to accumulate funds and to use them to finance strikes was fully recognized. Even to-day there is not complete unanimity, either in England or in France, regarding the extent to which Trade Unions should be free to use the strike as a political instrument. Indeed, conflict on this point has become at times more intense, and trade-union militancy in the industrial field more widespread. French Trade Unions have suffered from the general suspicion with which the State has regarded all associations. Their right to existence was recognized in 1884 and 1901, but in 1920 the Trade Union Confederation was theoretically prohibited, although no steps were taken to translate the theory into practice. Since the war, the legality of French Trade Unions has not been in dispute, but, up to 1963, the limits of the constitutional right to strike remained undefined, and they are still unclear.

Although Great Britain is traditionally more severe than France towards some manifestations of individual freedom—moral unconventionality, for example—both in peace-time and in wartime she has been more sympathetic towards the rights of groups and, in wartime, considerably more lenient towards the critics of Governmental policy. Wartime censorship in 1939 was much less rigid in England than in France, much more dependent on voluntary co-operation between press and officials. No doubt, as has been said, the long history of British security from invasion goes far to explain the differences of attitude. National character certainly plays a part, too, though it is not easy to decide where history ends and national character begins. British Protestantism, for example, has clearly been influenced by both. But, whatever the causes, the facts are undeniable.

Looking back, it is relatively easy to see how and why these

different attitudes arose. It is much more difficult to formulate
a satisfactory statement of the general principles which ought
reasonably to guide a Government in the exercise of its power
to tolerate or to repress the activities of individuals or groups
within its frontiers. In the first place, the reasons why the line
is, or has been, drawn at a particular place at a particular
time are always special reasons, dictated more by the pressure
of events than by abstract theories. In the second place,
history leaves its own scars on successive generations, so that,
even when the reason for a policy no longer exists, the attitude
of mind which approved it still persists. At the first sign of
troubled weather ahead, old national scars begin to ache.
Certain acts or attitudes have become symbolic of past dangers
or past victories and there is an automatic tendency to repeat
them in new circumstances.

In practice, there is a wide field of agreement, at least
between democratic States. Few States, for example, try to
regulate the choice of a marriage partner, the details of family
life, the kind of clothes people should wear or the time at which
they should eat or sleep. For the most part, people are free to
join what societies or clubs they want, without having to
worry about whether they are acting illegally or not. On the
other hand, few States to-day would leave parents in un-
restricted control of their children's lives, or would allow one
individual to act in such a way that he denied to others the
freedom of action that he claimed for himself. But this general
agreement on many points still leaves many others in which
there is no uniformity of practice as between States with
equal claims to be democratic, progressive and civilized. It is
difficult to imagine French citizens tolerating the restrictions
on the public consumption of alcoholic drinks which are
accepted in England, still less those imposed for a time by
prohibitionist America. Frenchmen often have fewer racial
prejudices than are met with in England and both French
and British citizens feel far less colour prejudice than is felt by
a South African white citizen, or an American. Norwegians

consider that income tax returns are of public interest, Britons that they are a private affair between themselves and the income tax officials. Belgians are shocked at the British habit of publishing details of testamentary dispositions. United States census returns require detailed information on all sorts of things which the average Briton considers of interest only to "snoopers". Great Britain recognizes the right to conscientious objection, even in wartime. France did not admit it until 1963. British law leaves the individual more freedom to decide how he shall bequeath his property than does French law.

Examples like this could be multiplied almost indefinitely. In the light of such evidence of human diversity, attempts like that of John Stuart Mill to find a general definition of the reasonable limits to State intervention and individual freedom must appear, for all practical purposes, virtually meaningless. "The sole end for which mankind are warranted, individually or collectively, in interfering with the liberty of action of any of their number," he wrote, " is self-protection". An individual, he thought, should not be restricted in any way, solely on the ground that it was for his own good. "There are good reasons for remonstrating with him," said Mill, "or reasoning with him, or persuading him, but not for compelling him." "The only part of the conduct of anyone, for which he is answerable to society, is that which concerns others. In the part which merely concerns himself, his independence is, of right, absolute. Over himself, over his own body and mind, the individual is sovereign."[1]

Mill goes on to make a number of reservations which only go to show how impossible it would be, in practice, for any State to try to apply this principle consistently. By "individuals", he means, he says, only "human beings in the maturity of their faculties." This, as we are only too painfully aware in this psychology-conscious age, is not a state susceptible

[1] Mill, *Utilitarianism, Liberty and Representative Government* (Everyman Edition, 1926), *On Liberty*, p. 73.

of clear definition, any more than is the point at which individual action ceases to have social repercussions. We can agree
on certain fairly easily recognizable extremes, but the number
of border-line cases will be infinite.

A contemporary writer provides a somewhat different
formula which, again, seems to create more problems than it
solves. Associations, he says, should "be subject to State
regulation in connection with those ends which only State
action can achieve." Otherwise, "the individual should be
free unless it can be shown in any particular case that State
action achieves a certain end better than voluntary combination."[1] How can we discover which are the ends that only
State action can achieve, or that State action can achieve
better? At one time, education was held to be a private affair;
twentieth-century England divides the responsibility between
public and private bodies, but opinion is divided as to how
far the State *ought* to go in granting or restricting the rights of
private educational bodies. The controversies created by
the 1974 Labour Government's proposal to "comprehensivize"
British education provide eloquent evidence of the difficulties in deciding where to draw the line between the rights
of the State and those of the individual. Similar difficulties
arose in 1975 and 1976 regarding the respective fields of
State and private medicine. When it comes to choosing
between a number of different combinations of State and
private control, who is to decide which is the best? Best for
whom? And in the opinion of whom?

A knowledge of the ways in which our own and other States
have answered questions like these will not necessarily bring
us nearer to finding satisfactory answers to-day, though it may
help. We can make up our minds only in the light of what we
feel are the ends that the State ought to be serving in its exercise of power. That must, therefore, be the next stage of our
enquiry.

---

[1] Mabbott, *The State and the Citizen* (Hutchinson's University Library), p. 126.

CHAPTER THREE

The Problem of Obedience

UP to now, what we have been considering are the *facts* of political organization; how, at different times and in different countries, men have regulated the relations between the State and themselves. We must now try to answer the more fundamental question: *Why* do they obey the State? It is one thing to affirm in general terms that without organization and rule society will degenerate into anarchy. It is quite another to assume that, because that is so, the individual feels it his duty to obey the particular Government of the State in which he finds himself. We know, in fact, that sometimes obedience ceases and there is a revolution. Is it possible to discover the reasons which have led men to feel that, as a general rule, they ought to obey their rulers, and those which to-day lead us, as citizens, to obey the State?

There is one simple and obvious answer to the question, Why do we obey the State? It is that we do so because we have no alternative. The State has the power to make us obey. There are always a number of people who are dissatisfied with the political system accepted by their countrymen. If only a small minority of these are prepared at any time to resort to revolution to change it, is not the explanation simply that they do not feel themselves strong enough to challenge the armed power of the State?

In the short run, this explanation is probably correct, but in the long run it does not take us very far. As MacIver has said: "Men have often acquired dominance with the aid of force, but none has kept the position thus acquired by sole reliance on this means?" If this view is accurate, and force is not enough, on what, then, do States rely? Why is obedience to the State the rule rather than the exception? Is it because we feel that we *ought* to obey, that to-day, no less than 2,000 years ago, it is our duty to "render unto Cæsar the things that are Cæsar's"? Why, at least in democratic States, do opposition parties reject revolution as a method of gaining power? Is it because they believe disobedience to be morally wrong, or merely politically inexpedient, or less likely in the long run to achieve their ends than constitutional methods? If the compulsion to obey is moral, then what makes us feel it? Is it inertia or conviction which leads us to accept the rule of established authority?

The problem of obedience is one of the most fundamental of all political problems. For, if we obey the State without question or protest, whether we do so from a sense of duty, from apathy or because we are convinced, rightly or wrongly, that obedience serves our interests, we are, by our obedience, acquiescing in, if not actively working for, the ends that the State exists to serve. As intelligent citizens we ought, therefore, to satisfy ourselves that we know what those ends are. If we question their rightness, we have then to go on to decide a further issue, namely, whether it is our duty to try to change those ends, and, if so, by what means. That will lead us to consider the conditions in which we should feel justified in continuing to obey and those in which we might hold disobedience to be either a right or a duty. In this chapter we shall discuss some of the reasons which persuade men that they ought to obey the State. In the next, we shall go on to discuss some of the implications of disobedience and the problems created by revolution.

It is easy enough to define the purpose of the State in terms of general principle. Over 2,000 years ago, Aristotle stated that man was "naturally a political animal" and that government was first formed "that we might live, but continued that we may live happily ". "It is evident," he said, "that all those Governments which have a common good in view are rightly established and strictly just." This definition would, no doubt, be acceptable to-day to the great majority of the citizens of democratic States. Neither Plato nor Aristotle, however, seriously contemplated the possibility that men might disagree irreconcilably both about the precise conditions that constitute "the good life", or "the common good", and about the methods that are most likely to create these conditions. Yet, in the twentieth century, it is precisely on these points, when we pass from the field of principle and definition to that of action, that men disagree most profoundly. The difficulties and disappointments crop up when we have to decide, not whether the purpose of the State is to promote the general welfare, but whether some actual State, our own or somebody else's, is in fact advancing towards the goal as fast as can reasonably be expected. "It is quite common," says Weldon, "for a body of men to be in complete agreement as to the kind of Government they want but to be violently at variance as to who shall be the governors and who the governed and we may all hold that rights given by the Constitution are sacred and still fight one another because we cannot agree as to what those rights are."

Because the political thinker is preoccupied with the particular problems of his age and country he can often see the problem of political obligation only through the spectacles of his own political fears or prejudices. And so he may present as a general doctrine, applicable to all societies, what is, in reality, a specific conclusion, applicable, if at all, only in the particular circumstances which led him to reach it. Thus, Hobbes, who was obsessed by the problem of order in the State, thought that the guarantee of order by a ruler constituted in itself a sufficient claim on the citizen's obedience. It did not occur to him that people might feel that some prices were too high to be paid even for such an essential requirement of civilized life, and prefer to risk their lives to obtain different conditions, rather than live them out in a so-called peace which made life for them not worth living. Religious feeling

and religious prejudices have also played their part in determining people's attitude to the problem of obedience. In the
seventeenth century many people held that it was part of
man's duty to God to obey the State. In England, for example,
Sir Robert Filmer argued that, since it was natural for mankind to be ruled by kings, it must have been so ordered by
God. God, he maintained, had entrusted the right to govern
to Adam and his descendants and Charles I had therefore
a divine right to govern, by virtue of his direct descent from
Adam.

To the modern student, there may seem to be a great many
obvious holes in this argument. For that matter, some of Sir
Robert Filmer's contemporaries thought that there were.
But if we stop and reflect for a minute, we shall admit that
many people to-day would affirm without feeling as much need
to prove their case as Sir Robert Filmer did, that, say, democratic republicanism, or constitutional monarchy, is the
"normal" or "right" form of government, because that is what
they are used to. One of the most eminent of Filmer's younger
contemporaries, the political philosopher, John Locke,
devoted a whole book to demolishing his arguments, point by
point, and another to explaining what were, in his own view,
the conditions of obedience. This latter work, the Second
Treatise on Civil Government, was published in 1690, when
Charles I had been beheaded and the revolution of 1688 had
already shown what the majority of British citizens thought
about the doctrine of divine right. Locke believed, and he
spoke for many of his contemporaries, that the government of
a country should be based on sounder principles. He tried,
therefore, to state afresh the reasons why men should obey a
monarch who had clearly been chosen not by God, but by
Whig politicians.

It is not necessary, however, to believe in the divine right
of kings in order to postulate links between obedience to the
State and obedience to God. The eighteenth-century Archdeacon Paley held that, "since God has attached arbitrary

rewards to beneficent and penalties to pernicious conduct, the wise man will take them into account."[1] The German philosopher, Kant, believed that men were under a moral obligation to obey the State, whether it brought them happiness or rewards or not. The early American Republicans of the Massachussets Colony thought that we ought to make sure that the State which we are expected to obey was ruled by men of whom God would approve, and that the way to be sure of this was to entrust government to Church members. They held that, since men are naturally evil, majority rule was logically bound to be the rule of the many bad over the few good.

Habit, too, has played its part in making up men's minds on this question. In the eighteenth century, the Scots philosopher, Hume, argued that, even if it were true that government must ultimately rest on consent, consent usually means little more than the acquiescence of inertia. "Obedience or subjection," he wrote, "becomes so familiar that most men never make any enquiry about its origin or cause, more than about the principle of gravity." Dr. Johnson believed that subordination to authority was not merely necessary to maintain order, but was something natural to mankind. "Every man," he said, "is born consenting to some system of government." Edmund Burke held that men ought to obey the State as they knew it, because it represented the accumulated wisdom of generations, and this accumulated wisdom of society must be presumed to be sounder than individual reasoning. The value of custom and tradition was emphasized by nineteenth-century British lawyers, like Austin and Sir Henry Maine, who saw obedience to the State as something customary and traditional, defined and crystallized—almost hallowed—by law.

Now, tradition and custom can constitute legitimate grounds for obedience only as long as we are convinced that they are good traditions and customs, or that tradition is good

---

[1] Carritt, *Morals and Politics* (Oxford University Press, 1935), p. 6.

in itself. If we hold that they represent so many examples, not of the accumulated wisdom, but of the accumulated follies of society, then the reasons for obedience disappear. Karl Marx adopted a different attitude towards the idea of habitual obedience. Trying to present a theory in which the idea of obedience to historical necessity took the place of obedience to what was right, or just, or expedient, or divinely ordained, he nevertheless often seemed to say—and certainly left many of his followers with the impression that he had said—that obedience to the mid-nineteenth-century capitalist State was a habit, and a bad habit. Society, as the Marxists saw it, was a conspiracy by the powerful few against the exploited many. It was a tyranny, established by force and perpetuated by guile. The oppressed classes obeyed the State only so long as they thought themselves powerless to resist it, or because they were tricked by propaganda into believing that they ought not to resist. Once they saw the true facts of the situation, they would unite and so become, together, powerful enough to throw off their chains.

Most of the theories mentioned up to now have one thing in common. They see the relationship between the citizen and the State as one over which the individual has little or no control. Obedience is conceived of as a product of either habit or duty or compulsion, and little or no attention is paid to the possibility that the citizen himself might take a hand in deciding the terms on which he will or will not agree to obey the State. From the sixteenth to the eighteenth century, however, European political thought came to be dominated by another set of theories, whose importance for us is precisely that they emphasized the need for obedience to be based on consent. At this stage, consent was thought of as the result of a bargain, or contract, between ruler and ruled. The theories are therefore known as contract theories.

A great deal of ink has been spilt in discussions as to whether, at some remote period of history or pre-history, there was ever an actual bargain or contract between rulers and people, or

whether the contractual relationship was a natural and inescapable element in human society. To us to-day, this argument seems totally unreal. To dismiss it in this way, however,
is to misunderstand the circumstances in which the idea of a
contract was born. And, as always in politics, some knowledge
of the circumstances is essential to a real understanding of
what was going on in men's minds at the time. One reason
why Locke's refutation of the doctrine of divine right and his
defence of the principles of 1688 carried weight was that he
was able to justify obedience in a way which men could accept
as part of the established order of the universe, as they had
previously accepted the doctrine of divine right. The strength
of this doctrine was precisely that it was held to be part of
the natural order of things, and so did not need to be thought
about or argued about. As soon as men began to challenge
the idea that obedience was the will of God, they were faced
with the need to find other reasons for obedience. It was only
natural that they should welcome a reason which could be
presented as something equally categoric, normal, inevitable
and right.

If, then, it could be satisfactorily established that obedience
was owed to the State by virtue of some explicit or tacit agreement between rulers and ruled, or between the ruled regarding
their ruler, then something like the old certainty could be built
up. Society inevitably presents a confused picture of competing
wills and conflicting opinions, but if it were possible to look back
to a time when social relationships were simple and primitive,
then we might discover the principles on which men have,
through the centuries, been consciously or unconsciously
basing their reasoning about the State. It was along these lines
that men argued. Since no records of these primitive times
existed, however, they were obliged to argue back from what
they knew of the nature of man to what they assumed must
have been his reactions at the beginning of civilization.

What is important in the concept of a social contract is the
conviction that it gave to men that the individual is, or can

be, the master of his fate. Obedience to the State is no longer
something ordained by God or by nature, but something
worked out by men, by virtue of which they promise, not
unconditional obedience, but obedience in return for certain
specific guarantees. It is a bargain, and therefore the individual
continues to owe obedience only as long as the terms of the
bargain are respected.

Of course, the idea that the citizen received something in
return for his obedience was not new. It was the essential
principle of feudalism, which gave protection and security to
the serf, in return for the services which he recognized as
owing to his feudal overlord. But when contract theories came
to the fore, feudalism had already given way to the mercantile
State, in which the monarch's powers were extensive and only
partially and incompletely controlled by Parliament. In 1593,
Queen Elizabeth reminded members of the House of Commons that they were not free "to speak everyone what he
listeth, or what cometh in his brain to utter that; but your
privilege is *aye* or *no*. . . ." In 1621, James I tore out of the
House of Commons Journal the page asserting the rights of
Members of Parliament to their traditional parliamentary
privileges. In 1649, Charles I lost his head because he refused
to admit that the King had not the right to set himself above
Parliament. But when William and Mary were offered the
throne after the revolution of 1688, it was only after they had
given specific assurances recognizing certain parliamentary
rights. Clearly, therefore, the theory of divine right was by
then discredited. Nevertheless, modern democracy was not
yet born. The idea of the contract helped men to make the
transition. It was a bridge between the notion of an absolute
ruler, responsible primarily, if not exclusively, to God, and
the conception, which was to be developed in the nineteenth
century, that Governments ought to be responsible to the
people through the medium of a democratically elected
Parliament.

The nature of the supposed bargain, or contract, determining the mutual obligations of sovereign and subjects,
varied considerably in the minds of different thinkers. Perhaps

because he lived in a period of civil war and personal insecurity, Hobbes saw peace and order as the basic needs of men. But he regarded men as being essentially incapable of living together peaceably, each man being an individualist whose conduct was determined by his need to satisfy his own desires. Since men differed and had incompatible desires, the natural consequence if they tried to live together in society would be conflict, "continual fear and danger of violent death". Or, as Sartre put it nearly 300 years later, "Hell is other people". The contract, or "covenant", must result from their recognition of their predicament (which Hobbes assumed to be possible, thanks to the fact that man is a thinking as well as a "willing" person), and from their decision to entrust to one authority, the sovereign (conceived of as either one man or an assembly), the right to make laws imposing the restrictions on individual liberty necessary for the peaceful existence of society.

It is easy enough to pick holes in this theory, if we look on the contract as a kind of basic constitution. How could we agree on the person, or persons, to be entrusted with these powers? Since the sovereign would have control of the armed forces, what could we do about it, if we believed that he was not doing what we had chosen him to do? Most contract theories, however, were not meant to be descriptions of actual or desirable forms of government, but rather attempts to analyse the essential nature and limits of obedience, given the the facts, or rather the assumptions, of the author about the nature of man.

Hobbes really assumed "that men are not born but are made sociable . . . that it is only as a creature subject to a discipline externally imposed, that man becomes moral".[1] Locke, however, regarded men as having naturally sociable instincts, and as being able and willing to learn to govern themselves. For him, therefore, the contract was a common undertaking to respect those laws of God and of nature which the community itself regarded as constituting the essential conditions of social life. In his view, the primary purpose of the contract was to protect property because the right to possess it was a natural or moral law, respect for which was the basis of

[1] Plamenatz, *Man and Society*, vol. 1, p. 154.

all civil society. "The great and chief end, therefore, of men uniting into commonwealths and putting themselves under government" he wrote, "is the preservation of their property; to which in the state of Nature there are many things wanting."[1]

It follows that, if power is entrusted to a ruler for certain definite ends, the measure of the obligation to obey must be the extent to which the ruler remains faithful to his trust. "For," says Locke, "all power given with trust for the attaining an end being limited by that end, whenever that end is mani-festly neglected or opposed, the trust must necessarily be for-feited, and the power devolve into the hands of those that gave it, who may place it anew where they shall think best for their safety and security."[2] He lays down four conditions for the exercise of power, which constitute, in his view "the bounds which the trust that is put in them (i.e., in the rulers) by the society and the law of God and Nature have set to the legis-lative power of every commonwealth, in all forms of govern-ment." They are, first to govern according to established laws, "not to be varied in particular cases, but to have one rule for rich and poor, for the favourite at Court, and the countryman at plough. Secondly: These laws also ought to be designed for no other end ultimately but the good of the people. Thirdly: They must not raise taxes on the property of the people without the consent of the people given by themselves or their deputies. Fourthly: Legislation neither must nor can transfer the power of making laws to anybody else, or place it anywhere but where the people have."[3]

This looks at first sight like good twentieth-century demo-cracy. But before the principles laid down by Locke can be put into practice, two questions have to be answered. Locke answered neither of them, precisely because, not being a twentieth-century democrat, he took for granted answers that we no longer take for granted to-day. First, he assumed that

---

[1] *Second Treatise on Civil Government*, § 124.   [2] *Ibid*, § 149.   [3] *Ibid.* § 142.

men would be able to agree on his proposed conditions, and so he does not consider what is likely to happen if a minority rejects the "original compact". "Every man," he says, "by consenting with others to make one body politic under one government, puts himself under an obligation to every one of that society to submit to the determination of the majority, and to be concluded by it, or else this original compact, whereby he with others incorporates into one society, would signify nothing, and be no compact if he be left free and under no other ties than he was in before in the state of Nature."[1] This is really nothing more than an assertion that if we are all agreed, or if the minority agrees to accept the verdict of the majority, the contract will be effective. Any agreement works so long as people stick to it. Merely to say, "As you were", if they do not, does not take us anywhere. What we want to know to-day, now that many of us can no longer assume that any system of government will necessarily receive general assent, is what is to happen if your contract is based on conditions that are incompatible with mine and neither of us will give way. Locke does admit the right of defence against an aggressor, against "whosoever uses force without right"—but he does not indicate how we are to judge that there *is* aggression, nor what is perhaps more important, who are to be the judges.

That brings us to the second question that Locke left unanswered. "The interest of the body of the people," as interpreted by the majority, presupposes the existence of political machinery through which "the people" can express their opinion. Locke speaks of the people "or their deputies". But he does not explain how we can be sure that the deputies really do speak for the people. He wrote in an age when elections for Parliament—and for Locke, Parliament, or "the legislative", as he calls it, is the supreme repository of power—were corrupt, when elected representatives belonged exclu-

---

[1] *Ibid.*, § 97

sively to the upper or upper middle classes, and when there
was not even a pretence of representation on a basis of population. It is true that he condemns corruption and maintains
that the people's representatives ought to be "freely chosen",[1]
but he was not profoundly interested in the machinery of
representation as we understand it to-day. By the term "the
people", he really meant those who actually sat in Parliament
at the time, and his vital concern was to prove that the supreme
power in the country should belong, not to the King, but to
Parliament—which, in effect, meant to the Parliament of
1688.

The fundamental difficulty about the contract theory is
that it explains why men obey the State, only if they do in fact
obey. It does not prove to those who refuse to obey where
they are wrong. It merely assumes that, in a rationally ordered
society, there would be sufficient agreement on fundamentals
for the minority to be able to submit to the will of the majority.
It does not provide a satisfactory explanation of obedience in
a State in which men are so profoundly divided in their aims
that for one side to submit to the other is to destroy the whole
purpose of life. Locke believed, for example, in religious
toleration and the right of private property. But what if the
religion of some forbids them to tolerate the existence of either
rival religions or private property? This difficulty did not
exist for Hobbes, because, in his analysis, once the sovereign
has been accepted, he decides for all and admits of no resistance. Plato resolved the dilemma by assuming that in the
ideal society a class of specially trained "experts" would
decide what was "right" or "best" for the community as a
whole. One can see traces of this attitude in the persistent
belief which exists in some quarters to-day that somehow,
somewhere, a body of "experts" can be discovered, who will
be free from bias and partisanship and so able to reach decisions on whatever is under discussion—economic policy, the

---

[1] *Ibid.*, § 222.

nationalized industries, or the European Economic Community
—purely on the merits of the case in question. It is an attitude
of mind which really evades the issue that we are trying to face,
because, like the contract theory, it assumes that some
fundamental unity really does exist, or is discoverable, if only
we are good or clever enough to find it. It does not help us to
decide what we ought to do if either of two (or some out of
many) rival philosophies may equally possibly be "right" or
"best" for the nation as a whole. We may be convinced in our
own minds that one is preferable to another. But that does
not necessarily blind us to the fact that others are equally
convinced in their minds that we are wrong and that there is
no way of choosing between us which is acceptable to all of
us as the "right" or the "best" way.

It was almost a century after the publication of Locke's
Treatise that the last and perhaps best-known exponent of the
contract theory tried to resolve the contradictions involved
in accepting both the contract theory and the fact of conflict
in society. Rousseau lived at a time when there were virtually
no checks on the power of the French king. In 1766, Louis XV
could still say: "Sovereign authority resides in my person
alone. . . . I alone possess legislative power. I depend on no
one and I share it with no one." The unity in the French
State in the eighteenth century came from the imposition of a
single will. Rousseau believed that primitive men had been
born free. The growth of society and State had left them
"everywhere in chains". He sought in the Social Contract
an instrument which would enable them to recover both
their freedom and their equality. His contract is, therefore,
something far more revolutionary than Locke's. It demands,
as does that of Hobbes, the surrender of the individual will
to a sovereign. But for Rousseau the sovereign is the whole
community of which the individual is himself a constituent
part and over whose activities he has the same degree of control as all the rest of his fellow citizens. The contract is really,
in Rousseau's opinion, between two aspects of the individual.

"Each, giving himself to all, gives himself to nobody." Men are at one and the same time, "a passive body of subjects and an active body of sovereigns." "The Government exists by grace of the sovereign and its power can be resumed or divided at will by the sovereign."[1] And the sovereign is the people, the sum of individuals acting as a community.

Since all decisions affecting the community are taken by the individuals themselves who make up the community, it does not at first sight seem clear why there is any need for a contract at all. But it is here that Rousseau uses the contractual idea to solve the problem created by the recognition that there are conflicts between the wills of some and the wills of others. He does not, like Locke, think in terms of a majority will, but in, terms of a "general" will, which represents, not a compromise between conflicting wills, but what is common to the community as a whole, the "real" purpose of the community, considered as a single entity and not as a sum of individuals. The contract is an undertaking whereby the individual, in sacrificing his individual will to that of the community, renounces the right to act in a way dictated by selfish or individual purposes, in that sphere of conduct where his acts affect the community. His decisions are determined henceforth not by his personal interests, but by those of the community as a whole. The acts of the community which are taken as a result of these decisions are therefore expressions of the "general" or "real" will of the community. We shall discuss later the theoretical difficulties involved in the concept of a general will. But, even if we accept for the moment the validity of this part of Rousseau's argument, we should find ourselves confronted with a host of difficulties if we tried to translate it into terms of practical politics. First, it is useful only if it is, in actual fact, possible for a community to recognize when its acts are expressing the general will and when they are not. Rousseau himself was conscious of this difficulty. "Has the body politic," he asked, "any specific

---

[1] *The Social Contract*, Preface by Ernest Barker, p. xlvi (The World's Classics, 1947).

organ which may serve to give form to its will?" He never answered this question very satisfactorily. He thought of States on the model of Geneva or the Greek City State, small enough for a body of citizens to govern themselves by a kind of mass meeting. Even if it were possible to envisage modern government in this way, we should still have to assume, if Rousseau's conditions were to be met, that the citizens were all possessed of articulate political convictions. Huntsmen may be genuinely convinced that the fox likes being hunted, but how can they know that the fox shares this view, unless he can speak for himself? Even if we assume that we are all equally capable of reaching independent conclusions, we still have to find a way of recognizing when we are really considering the general interest and when we only think that we are. I may quite genuinely believe that what suits *my* purpose would also be best for *you*, but may I not be led to that conclusion by selfishness, of which I am completely unaware, and which I am therefore unable to correct?

Rousseau himself perceived that in the real world he was unlikely to meet with the conditions in which his Social Contract could function properly and so he introduced a compromise in the shape of the "legislator", whose function is to help citizens to find the right road. "The People always desire the good but, left to themselves, they do not always know where it lies."

This device really solves nothing. It is as difficult to imagine an all-wise legislator or leader as it is to imagine an infallible electorate (or body of citizens, for Rousseau did not think in terms of elected representatives.) We are still left with the problem that Locke left us with. He assumed that, in their hearts, men agree on certain fundamental principles; Rousseau assumed that if they were properly trained they could learn to agree. We are still faced with the problem of deciding on what grounds we can claim obedience to a State when we can discover no way of eliminating conflicts on fundamental principles. If I refuse to obey on the ground that the Government seems to me to be acting neither in my interests nor in those of the community as a whole, who is to decide which of us, I or the Government, is the true representative of the "real" will of the community? We are both interested parties, and in sovereign States, which are the only ones we are considering at the moment, there is no objective outsider with undisputed authority, to whom both sides can submit the problem.

The eighteenth and early nineteenth centuries saw the generalization of two new ideas which led to a different approach to the problem. The first was the belief in human equality proclaimed by the constitution-makers of both the American and French Revolutions. "We hold these truths to be self-evident," said the American Declaration of Independence in 1776, "that all men are created equal." And thirteen years later, the first article of the French Declaration of the Rights of Man affirmed that "Men are born and remain free and equal." The American Declaration included among men's fundamental and inalienable rights the right to the pursuit of happiness.

These two beliefs, the belief in human equality and in the right to happiness, transformed men's attitudes towards the problem of obedience to the State. The seventeenth century Puritans had seen life, if not as "nasty, brutish and short", at least as a vale of tears through which men passed in their search for eternal salvation. Human souls might be equal before God, but that gave human beings no right to claim equal political rights on earth. Once people came to believe that men were of equal worth here and now as well as in the hereafter, that they had an equal right to conditions which made life worth living in their own judgment, they soon came to believe, too, that they must be of equal worth to the State and therefore that they ought to have an equal right to decide what made them happy.

This conclusion, like the earlier ones that we have discussed, was not easy to put into practice. It raised two major questions in people's minds. First, if the happiness of some is attainable only at the cost of the unhappiness of others, who is to decide which shall have priority? If my meat is your poison, and we can have only one dish, who decides which dish we are to have? Second, what are we to do if what makes some people happy seems to others to be morally wrong?

Of course, we can get out of the first difficulty if we make the familiar assumption that there is some essential harmony in the universe, if only we can discover it. The nineteenth century produced its own variant on this theme. Just as, in the seventeenth and eighteenth centuries, men believed that there were natural laws determining what was right or just, so in the nineteenth there were men who assumed that natural laws could produce universal happiness. Adam Smith, whose ideas dominated much of nineteenth century thought, argued that an economic system in which individuals were all pursuing their own selfish and often conflicting interests would still produce, by some beneficent law of God or nature, a happy and harmonious community. Another way out of the difficulty was to postulate some kind of political machinery which would enable the community to decide what made people happy. This approach is in line with that of Rousseau, but if he never devised any satisfactory machinery for ascertaining the will of the community, later thinkers could devise no satisfactory way of proving whether the machinery that they devised had, or had not, produced the desired result. The nineteenth-century German philosopher, Hegel, turned the problem inside out. He saw the State as the creator rather than the product of men, in the sense that only in society could men discover their own moral values and so realize their full potentialities. Naturally some States and some societies are better than others. But since Hegel assumed that the evolution of society was one of progress towards the good, he postulated the ultimate attainment of an ideal system in which the rational individual would be free, because he would be in complete harmony with the will expressed by the laws and conventions of an ideal State. The problem of obedience would then no longer exist, for in the ideal State the Government would always represent the real will of the community.

This is a brief and oversimplified summary of one of the most complex and confusing arguments ever presented to his readers by a political writer. The argument is rendered even more confusing by Hegel's habit of using words, at times, as Humpty-Dumpty did, to mean what he chose them to mean. One result was that it was not always clear whether he was discussing real men in the real world or ideal men in the ideal world. He sometimes seemed to be claiming that the citizen should always obey the State.

What he was anxious to emphasize, however, was that State and citizen are inseparable and that each moulds the other until they reach full development in harmony. Not all those who believed that the State represented, or could represent, the true interests of a society argued in this way. The nineteenth-century English philosopher, T. H. Green, came to the conclusion that, if the State did not succeed in winning the allegiance of the individual, then the fault lay in all probability with the State. "It is a sign," he said, "that it is not a true State; that it is not fulfilling its primary function of maintaining law equally in the interest of all, but is being administered in the interest of classes." In other words, where Hegel had seemed to conclude that the citizen was not being a true citizen, Green decided that the State was not being a true State.

Theories which assume the existence of a community will or spirit—organic theories as they are called—whether their intention is autocratic or democratic, have in common the belief that a society possesses a personality of its own, that it differs in some way from the sum of the individuals comprised in it. They believe that, as A. D. Lindsay put it, "there is something which can be called a general will because there is something which can be called a common mind. . . . When men who are working together pool their experiences and share their difficulties, there can and often does come out of their discussions a decision which is really the decision of the society, which no individual could have come to of himself, and which each yet recognizes as more completely carrying out the purposes of society than his own original suggestion.''[1]

This view has a good deal to recommend it. Groups do behave in ways which are often not characteristic of the behaviour of their members, considered individually. There is such a thing as mass hysteria. A Quaker meeting does, as many Quakers have testified, produce among its members a like-mindedness, a unity of purpose, which they recognize as an emanation, or a creation, of the group. In other words, the group can, and often does, contribute to the formation of the individual mind and character, just as the individual makes his contribution to the group. Two heads are better than one— not merely twice as good, but qualitatively better, in the sense that they can produce results that neither head could ever have thought of singly. In wartime, groups of men can reach heights of heroism far beyond anything that the members of it would have been capable of if they had acted singly, precisely because each man helps to strengthen the group and is, in turn, strengthened by it.

It is not easy, however, to translate this consciousness of the group entity into political terms. We must beware of jumping to conclusions which may be based on false analogies. Is the State a group in the same sense as, say, a Quaker meeting? Are there not significant differences? The groups that we have been discussing are united either by a common purpose or by a common attitude to certain problems. A State is a large, heterogeneous collection of people, most of whom know nothing of the lives or purposes of most of the others. It consists of a number of groups with apparently conflicting aims and outlooks, none of which has *chosen* to

---

[1] Quoted in Carritt, *Morals and Politics* (Oxford University Press, 1935), p. 204.

belong to the particular State to which they do belong. It may be that the community sense is present only when there is some unity of purpose. For many people, the existence of disunity of purpose is an inescapable reality in the world as we know it, and the identity of interests or the unity of purpose, which is the characteristic of the general will, is merely an ideal which men have assumed to be, or which they hope one day may be, attainable. If we accept this conclusion, it is not possible to take a problematical "general will" into account in trying to decide why and when we ought to obey the State.

The majority of nineteenth-century political thinkers, in Britain at any rate, were unable to believe in the concept of the general will. The great social and legal reformer, Jeremy Bentham, elaborated, just over a century ago, a theory of political obligation which assumed, not only that human desires did conflict, but that, as far as we knew, they always would do so. He believed that the purpose of government was to make men happy. He accepted the assumption that men were equal and therefore that they had an equal right to decide for themselves what kind of government would obtain happiness for them. As their views would inevitably conflict, it followed that they would not all be able to have what they wanted. But if we were to add up all the individual wishes expressed (each man counting for one), then the opinion expressed by the majority would represent the maximum happiness attainable in the circumstances.

This approach has all the attraction of simplicity and seems at first sight to provide a practical solution to all the difficulties encountered hitherto. It has an answer to both the questions which were raised by the acceptance of the principles of equality and of the right to happiness. If everyone cannot be happy, then priority is given to the majority, which means that as much happiness is created as the facts will allow. If we want incompatible things, I shall get my way if there are more people in the State who think as I do than who think as you do. This principle holds even if, for many of us, what makes the majority happy seems morally wrong. For Bentham, the only criterion of political rightness was numerical. If we are all equal, there is no way of deciding which of us is "right". If you and I disagree, all we can do is to ensure that the State's policy shall reflect the conclusions of the majority as to what is "right". "The happiness of the worst man of the species," he wrote, "is as much an integrant of the whole mass of human happiness as is that of the best man." There is no need to make distinctions between ideal and non-ideal States, between what the individual thinks he wants and what is in his real interest. The "general will" is an abstraction. What we have to deal with in real life are individuals, every one different from every other. If we ask each one what he wants and tot up the answers, the result is mathematically bound to tell us what will give all of them the maximum satisfaction achievable in the circumstances. The purpose of the State is to produce this satisfaction, or social utility. We obey the State because it is in our interest to obey, because any other type of organization would provide us with *less* satisfaction than would this system. There is no way of determining what is in our best interests by invoking some problematical mystical or ideal unity. We all have an equal voice in deciding the matter, since there is no objective certainty, and we record our decision in the form of so many million concrete votes, representing our choice as to who shall govern us and how.

Not all Bentham's contemporaries could accept this simple and revolutionary "utilitarian" philosophy. John Stuart Mill, for example, could not accept the idea that happinesses were things that could be added up in this simple way, like quantities of merchandise. "It is better," he said, "to be a human being dissatisfied than a pig satisfied; better to be Socrates dissatisfied than a fool satisfied."[1] He was conceivably right,

---

[1] *Utilitarianism, op. cit.*, p. 9.

but the task of devising political machinery that could take adequate account of the difference between the two sorts of happiness is certainly beyond us at our present stage of political evolution. How much more would one kind of happiness be worth, in, say, votes? The answer is, surely, that the State can work only through institutions and that no institutions that human beings have so far devised have been able to discover a standard by which qualitative differences can be measured. It is easy to say that some people are capable of more happiness than others, that their political judgment is sounder, their sense of responsibility deeper, their understanding of political issues more profound. Until we have found a way of translating these differences into institutional terms, they must remain irrelevant for political purposes. The only practical way that we have discovered of recognizing politically our fundamental equality as human beings, however much we may differ in character or aptitudes, is to let each of us count for one, but to do all that we can to see that to innate inequalities, which we cannot do anything about, we do not add inequalities of opportunities to make the best of ourselves, where we can do something to equalize them.

It is here that Bentham's utilitarianism is guilty of unrealistic over-simplification. "One man one vote" can give us an accurate estimate of the distribution of political opinions, only when men are more or less equally capable of knowing what they want and of expressing their opinions clearly, and when, in addition, they have efficient technical means of recording those views. If I vote for X because he stands for peace with the Soviet Union, you vote for Y because he stands for resistance to Soviet aggression, one of your neighbours votes for X because he is in favour of an increase in engineers' wages and another for Y because he is not, while friends of yours vote respectively for Z because he is opposed to the tyranny of State control, for X because he is in favour of increasing old age pensions, for Y because he believes in fair shares, for Z because he wants to reduce your Income Tax, and for none of

them because none of them will support the campaign for
unilateral nuclear disarmament, what does it all add up to?
If Y is elected, it may be for anything from ten to ten thousand
different reasons. It is quite possible for the same candidate,
and certainly for a number of candidates representing the
same policy, to be elected by voters who want higher wages,
lower prices, strong defence forces, higher old age pensions, a
reduction in Income Tax, more exports and more goods for
the home market. Yet no candidate can logically support all
or even most of these.

What this argument amounts to is that the electorate can
vote for things which are incompatible with each other,
because it is not a single collective mind, capable of sorting
out incompatibilities, but a sum of separate individual
decisions. Even the individual, moreover, cannot always sort
out the incompatibilities. Electors vote for policies that are
incompatible because they do not realize that they are
incompatible. They may vote for policies that they do not
approve of, because their dominant interest is better represented by a candidate who does 'not agree with them on anything else, and so they choose to sacrifice some things for
others. They may vote for a candidate because they think
they agree with him and then find that they do not, or that
they have been misled as to his real views. In complex modern
systems, electors are not asked what policy would make them
happy. They are confronted with two or three candidates
whose policies are more or less laid down in advance and asked
which of the three they are prepared to put up with.

In the twentieth century we are much less sure than
Bentham was that the uniqueness and complexity of human
wishes can be reduced to a simple *Yes* or *No*, for or against.
We do not know whether a party which obtains a majority at
a general election is actively approved of by the electorate or
chosen as the least of the available evils. We do not often know
what the majority is for, even if we know *whom* it is for, because
we have no accurate way of assessing the relative values

attached by different sections of the electorate to different items of the programme. Modern democracy has concentrated its attention rather on the other requirement, namely, that electors shall, at least, be equally well equipped to use the information and the machinery available to them in making their choice. The twentieth century social service State tries to make sure that all citizens have equal access to the facts which ought to influence their decision, that education is general enough to enable them all to follow what is going on, and that opportunities for them to play their part as citizens are such that no individual is discriminated against by reason of poverty, ill-health, race or religion. How far it has been successful in this aim is something that will have to be discussed in later chapters.

The application of the majority principle raises another important problem which Bentham did not solve, namely: What is to happen to the minority? It is not enough to argue that if the majority get their way there are more happy than unhappy people. More happy people does not necessarily mean more happiness. It all depends on *how* happy they are. It is when we come to think about the minority that we can usefully take into account John Stuart Mill's qualitative distinction. For the degree of unhappiness that the minority has to endure, by virtue of the fact that its wishes are to be ignored, may well affect the quality of the happiness looked forward to by the majority.

There are practical as well as altruistic reasons why a majority is rarely well advised to leave the views of the minority out of account. If we ask *why* the minority agrees to obey a State whose purpose is demonstrably not to further their happiness but to deny it, the reply of the average British citizen, with centuries of Parliamentary government behind him, will be the common sense one that that state of affairs is not necessarily permanent, that perhaps in the near future the tables will be turned and to-day's minority become to-morrow's majority. In the meantime, government must go on, and it can do so only on condition that both sides agree to accept certain rules. As long as there is a reasonable chance that the minority will be able to convert enough people to give them a majority in a not too far distant future, it is clearly to their advantage to stick to the rules that they would like their opponents to respect when *they* are in the minority. Such an answer can be given in Great Britain, where there is a substantial area of common ground among members of the democratic parties regarding the way in which a political system should function, and where there is substantial confidence that any party in power will respect certain rights generally agreed to be essential in a democracy. Let us suppose, however, that a Labour party programme were to include, let us say, proposals for the suppression of the Catholic Church, the Liberal party and Women's Suffrage. Does anyone imagine that this programme, even if it obtained a majority, which is inconceivable in itself, could ever be applied without encountering the active opposition of the defeated minority? If we ask why a minority should obey the State, we must answer surely that it will not necessarily do so if the majority abuses its power. The majority principle can function where there is a substantial area of agreement about the foundations of society, or where, in the absence of agreement, the disputants are prepared to do as they would be done by. In 1927, Lord Balfour said of the British system of government that "it is evident that our whole political machinery presupposes a people so fundamentally at one that they can safely afford to bicker; and so sure of their own moderation that they are not disturbed by the never-ending din of political conflict. May it always be so."[1]

If the first half of his sentence is less true to-day, it is essential to the survival of the system that the second half should continue to be true. For the minority, the problem of

[1] Preface to Bagehot, *The English Constitution*.

obedience is satisfactorily soluble only with the co-operation of the majority. Bentham took it for granted that the minority would be willing to co-operate in carrying out the will of the majority. But what interest has a minority in obedience if it is offered only the satisfaction of seeing the happiness of others? Marx called on the workers to revolt because he was convinced that only by revolt could they throw off their chains. If a State wants to ensure obedience, not only from those whose purposes it exists to serve, but also from those whose purposes it must deny, then it must see to it that, on balance, it is more in the interests of the minority to obey than to disobey. In other words, it must offer some alternative to revolution, by which the minority can hope to become a majority. Modern democracies have interpreted these claims by the minority to the tolerance or good will of the majority as including at least an equal right to present their case to the electorate, and the right to enjoy as much happiness as is compatible with the carrying out by the representatives of the majority of their undertakings to the electorate. Since Bentham's day, the concept of equality of rights, not only as between individuals, but also as between groups and between majority and minority, has become susceptible of almost indefinite reformulation. In his day, attention was concentrated on the equal right of citizens to record their vote, which meant that the franchise had to be reformed and extended. The next step was to educate all citizens, at least so that they were literate enough to play their full part in political life. The secrecy of the ballot had to be guaranteed, so that no individual was intimidated in his choice. Social services made it possible for the poorer citizen to compete on more equal terms with the rich for posts of responsibility in the State. Groups within the State obtained the right to propagate minority views, even when they were abhorrent to the majority. The constitutional right of the minority to criticize the majority was symbolized in the title: "His (or Her) Majesty's Opposition."

This process of evolution is still going on. We may not agree any more in the twentieth than men did in the seventeenth—or even in the fourth century B.C.—on absolute values. We may be no nearer to answering the question: What is right? We have certainly gone much farther than any preceding century in our attempt to give every citizen equal possibilities of making up his own mind and of deciding whose views of what is right are to prevail. In democratic States, at least, citizens to-day can decide what kind of State they want to obey and the terms on which they will promise obedience.

CHAPTER FOUR

The Problem of Change

IT is evident from what has been said so far that the history of civilized States is one in which the relations between Government and citizen are perpetually changing. Sometimes the changes have come about gradually, almost imperceptibly, sometimes as a result of the "explosive eruption of pent-up forces" that we call revolution. What we, as citizens, have to decide is: first, whether it can ever be right to use the revolutionary method to induce changes, and, if so, in what circumstances; second, what we feel ought to be the attitude of the State towards revolutionaries, or potential revolutionaries; and third, what are the practicable alternative methods of social change.

It is necessary to be clear, first of all, on what we mean by the term revolution. In ordinary language, the word is often used to describe both the method of inducing change and the scope of the changes. In this wider sense, it means, as MacIver has said, "to embrace decisive changes in the character of Government, even though they do not involve the violent overthrow of an established order." The revolution of 1688, for example, was a peaceful revolution and, although the Crown changed hands, legislative power remained in the hands of the great Whig families and was used for much the same ends as before. In the narrower sense, the word revolution refers exclusively to the methods used to bring about particular changes in the system of government. It leaves out of account what the revolution is about, who are the revolutionaries, and how far they are successful in achieving their ends. The emphasis is on the use of violence, or extra-constitutional means, involving a temporary breakdown of the system which is being challenged and its replacement by another system or constitution. The French Revolution replaced the arbitrary rule of an absolute monarch by the rule of an elected Assembly. The Russian revolutions of 1917 changed the entire personnel and purpose of government. They sought to substitute for the autocratic rule of the Czars first, a Socialist State, then the rule of the Communist Party, in the name of the workers. The social and economic legislation of the British Labour Government of 1945 to 1950 was sometimes called a social revolution. Its declared aim, too, was the establishment of a Socialist State. But in the sense in which we are using the word, the French and the Russian Governments were, and the Labour Government was not, revolutionary. The former established their Governments by force; while the latter sought to achieve its purpose through the normal constitutional machinery. Similarly, though the economic changes which resulted in the development of capitalism in the nineteenth century are described as an industrial revolution, and though they modified the relations between the different classes of society no less profoundly than did either the Russian revolution or the British Labour Government's legislation in the twentieth century, they do not constitute a revolution in this narrower sense of the term. There was no challenge to the established system of Government, and the modifications in the political system which the economic changes rendered inevitable were introduced gradually and constitutionally.

In this sense, then, revolution is, in Laski's phrase, "an attempt by the use of force against the Government legally in power to compel a change in what are held to be, by those using such force, the actual purposes of the State." Such an attempt may be described as a conspiracy, a *coup d'état*, a *putsch*, a rebellion, a riot, a mutiny, a palace revolution, according to its political or emotional colouring. It may be successful or abortive, it may or may not be accompanied by civil war and prolonged interruption of government, and it may or may not be followed by a period of consolidation in which all opposition to the revolutionary policy is more or less forcibly suppressed. It may be brought about by an individual, a class, a religious sect, or a political party. It may aim at far-reaching and fundamental changes in the whole complex of relations between the citizen and State, or it may look no further than the seizure of power from the actual holders of it. Thus some South American revolutions have been merely transfers of power from one General to another, while the French and Russian revolutions transferred power from one class to another. The German Nazi and the Italian Fascist revolutions, although they made use of constitutional machinery to present a façade of constitutionalism, were essentially revolutions, in the sense that the threat of force prevented the constitutional machinery from working in the way that it was intended to work and so enabled the leaders of the revolutionary party to take control of the machinery themselves. The essential element in the definition is the use against the established Government of force, in the sense of pressure not provided for as part of the normal working of existing institutions.

We have seen that individualism, with its emphasis on the rights of the majority, and idealist or organic theories, with their emphasis on the fundamental community of interests in a society, both fail to satisfy those who, consciously at least, feel themselves out of harmony with the purposes pursued by the State. It is doubtful whether a minority derives much comfort either from the Benthamite argument that the sacrifice of their interests, however regrettable, is necessary to ensure the achievement of the maximum attainable happiness, or from the idealist assumption that their best interests will be served by the application of policies assumed to represent the will of the community as a whole. It is easy to understand, therefore, that a minority may rebel and seek to impose its will. It is less easy to determine in what precise circumstances a revolution is likely to break out, or when, in the view of the observer, it is justified in principle or likely to succeed in practice. It is obvious from the most cursory knowledge of history that disobedience does not always, or even generally, occur at a time when the rebels are confident of success. There are individuals who stand out against the State knowing that they cannot succeed and will probably pay for their disobedience with their lives. There are conscientious objectors who are prepared to pay the penalty of disobedience whatever it may be. History can point to many small bands of men who, united by a common purpose, have been prepared to defy the State in what, to any outside observer, and probably often to themselves, appeared to be hopeless causes. There were the agrarian Communists in seventeenth century England, the Protestants of South-West France in the seventeenth and eighteenth centuries, the Mormons in America in the nineteenth century. In a modern democracy, the practical advantages of revolution appear to be few. A small minority can rarely hope to succeed, and the larger it becomes, the greater the likelihood that it will be able to achieve its ends by constitutional means. It is in systems which contain no provision, or inadequate provision, for constitutional change, that revolution may become a logical necessity.

Even then, however, even though the revolutionaries believe in their cause and are convinced that they have no alternative to revolution, there are preoccupations which may deter them from entering upon the hazardous adventure of revolution. For a revolution is precisely that. History can provide us with innumerable examples of the fact that nothing is more unpredictable than the course of a revolution. Once the "explosive" forces have been released, no one can estimate the extent of the resultant upheaval. The first item on the revolutionary programme is to gain power in order to change the system. The second is to keep it long enough to ensure the stability of the new system. Some revolutions never get beyond this stage, for the conquest of power reveals itself as so difficult that, from a means, it becomes transformed into an end in itself.

Even if a revolution does not miscarry in its early stages, it is bound to go through a troubled period when the revolutionaries, who were united in their determination to get rid of a régime, discover that they are less united when it comes to putting another one in its place. This happened in France in 1848. Then again, social habits are very deeply rooted and often harder to change than ideas. It is possible for people to feel enthusiasm for generous ideals, even to support a revolution inspired by them, without grasping the extent to which the revolution will affect their own lives. Even when the majority of the population are willing to undergo the personal discomforts entailed by social transformation, with the best will in the world, it takes time to adapt to changed circumstances. As Léon Blum wrote: "The results of great revolutionary changes are never consolidated all at once. Equilibrium is re-established bit by bit, and that, indeed, is how nature imposes *a posteriori* upon revolutions the rules that would normally have applied to a more normal evolution."[1]

This limitation can be most clearly seen in the Russian revolution which tried to turn a backward—indeed feudal— economy into a modern industrial State almost overnight. As one writer has said: "You can produce tractors and tanks by a Five-Year Plan, but you cannot produce an administrative class so easily."[2] The French revolution attempted to give France a constitution, or rather, a number of revolutions gave her a whole series of constitutions. But constitutions need more than political ideals to make them work. They need settled traditions of constitutional government, and these can be built up only slowly. That is why, although revolutions may sometimes be inevitable, or even necessary—and Léon Blum for one has argued that the revolutionary method of change *is* sometimes necessary—"in the end, revolutions do not save

[1] *For All Mankind* (Gollancz, 1946), p. 43.
[2] Crossman, *op. cit.*, p. 53.

time." Their pace is inescapably determined by the rate at which the mass of the population is ready to change its habits. They may even lose time. For when equilibrium, stable or unstable, is reached, after a more or less prolonged period of violence or upheaval, it may not be at all what the revolutionaries had hoped for. The revolutionary short cut may turn out to be not even the longest way home, but not a way home at all. In the tumult and disturbance, men can lose sight of their objective and concentrate their energies on the primary need to restore order, only to discover that, by the time order has been restored, new forces have come into prominence, either opposed to the revolutionary leaders, or endeavouring to move faster than they are prepared to move, or in directions not entirely the same. The ensuing conflict often results in an uneasy compromise. Sometimes the revolution is side-tracked and the original objective remains almost as remote as it seemed before the revolution occurred. Sometimes new obstacles have presented themselves, making the way back to the main road even more difficult than were the first stages of the journey. Once launched, a revolution may become impossible to control, because new and unforeseen emergencies have to be met and how and where the leaders will lose their way are equally unpredictable. The explosive force does not exhaust itself all at once. There is always a danger from unexploded bombs during the difficult transition years.

Something of the difficulties likely to be encountered can perhaps be conveyed by a brief reference to the difficulties that France experienced during the transition from occupation to liberation. True, this was not a revolution, but some of the difficulties were similar. Indeed, a revolution might have rendered them insuperable. France emerged from the occupation in 1944 with a fundamental cleavage in the State between resisters and those who had collaborated with the enemy. She faced a formidable task of reconstruction, calling for great political and administrative skill. That task would have been easier if the leaders who had brought her to liberation had also been the most fitted to carry on from there. But the qualities required were totally different. It is an unfortunate but inescapable fact that the capacities to lead a *maquis* resistance group bear no relationship to those required to administer a Government department or a municipality, and that a resister who blows up a bridge or part of the railway track is usually less qualified to rebuild them than a collaborator who happens also to be a constructional engineer. The first five post-war years saw a more or less painful return to normal, in which all but a handful of resisters who happened also to have the requisite qualities for reconstruction dropped out of sight and all but a handful of collaborators whose record was peculiarly distasteful resumed their normal occupations. This readjustment was possible in France, though it was not easy, precisely because the situation was not revolutionary. In the hypersensitive atmosphere of revolution, new leaders who feel themselves challenged by groups with differing conceptions of either objectives or methods are likely to suppress them or to be themselves submerged by them. Either the purposes of the original revolution are lost sight of in a series of subsequent revolutions, or the original leaders maintain themselves in power by a vigorous repression of any criticism which might encourage the emergence of rival claimants for power. Ultimately, there is inevitably a loss of contact between the rulers and those who were the source of their inspiration and so, for good or ill, the course of the revolution is changed.

History provides us with numerous examples of revolutions whose original objective was only partially reached, or not reached at all. The French revolutionaries did not dream that the path they took in 1789 would lead them, five years later, to Thermidor. Lenin's aim was to bring into being the Marxist classless society, in which Marx had assumed that the State would wither away. The Soviet State is far more powerful than ever the Czarist State was, and new classes have arisen to replace those of the Czarist régime. Stalin stated that there was no likelihood of the State's withering away. Like the Red Queen in *Alice Through the Looking-Glass*, some revolutionary States use up so much of their energy in keeping in the same place, that they have none left with which to get somewhere else.

There is a moral as well as a practical argument against revolution. It is possible to argue, and most democracies do argue in this way, that in politics the means cannot be divorced from the end, and that revolution is a bad means. If, as many people believe, it is morally wrong to use violence to achieve power, then it follows that we are not justified in doing evil that good may come. Still, even if we accept the view that revolution is misguided, or even morally wrong, that does not necessarily give us the right to deny other people's right to resort to it. If we believe that the authority of the State is founded in the last resort on the consent of the individual conscience, then we prevent the free expression of individual wills only at the risk of defeating our own ends as surely as by revolution. We are laying ourselves open to charges similar to those which we have just made against revolutionaries. If intolerance is a bad preliminary to revolutionary government, surely it is also a bad habit for a democracy claiming to apply the principle of human equality. If a potential revolutionary remains unconvinced by the preceding argument against revolution, is he, then, to be forced to be sensible and moral? If not, how is his freedom to revolt to be reconciled with the obligation of a democratic State to maintain law and order in accordance with the wishes of the majority?

The problem of revolution in a democratic State is the problem of reconciling the need to save the State's soul with the equally pressing need to save its body. In practice, democracies have resolved this dilemma only by evading the issue. To many supporters of democracy this is one of its chief merits. What matters in problems like this is not so much logic as common sense. It is less important to face the issue than to recognize that we are dealing with principles which, if pushed to their logical conclusions, are irreconcilable. Democracies endeavour, therefore, to avoid deciding irrevocably for or against one or the other and tend to count on citizens to refrain from putting them in a position where such a choice becomes inevitable. To anti-democrats, this eternal search for a compromise which fully satisfies nobody is held to be a vice and, of course, democrats are also aware that it can become one. In practice, democracies have generally dealt with the dilemma presented by the existence of revolutionary forces within a State by assuming that neither side will push the other too far. They recognize that political loyalties are not the only ones, that even individuals who accept the general argument that revolution is both futile and wrong may still not be able to accept the alternative which the State offers them, because it may appear to them to be even more wrong. For example, a conscientious objector may be convinced that resistance to war is practically ineffective, dangerous to the survival of a State whose general purposes he approves of and, even, morally wrong, but still feel that it is God's will that he shall not fight in any circumstances, whatever the consequences may be.

In such cases, democracies often, though not always, recognize that there can be no absolute or *a priori* determination of right or wrong and that only the extremes are clear. If minority interests are unduly sacrificed to those of the majority then there is a risk that the minority will revolt against a majority which denies them adequate self-expression. On the other hand, to give free rein to the expression of individual wills, where these are in conflict, is to risk anarchy or civil war, the dissolution of the State itself. All that the State can do is to remain alert to both dangers and resolve the dilemma pragmatically, by trying to strike a balance between the conflicting opinions. In practice, individual protests are usually tolerated, provided that they are not likely to prevent the expression of the will of the majority. Conscientious objection, for example, has been recognized in Great Britain, partly because the State is genuinely anxious not to suppress the right of the individual conscience to make itself heard, but partly also because conscientious objectors are not numerous enough to endanger national defence. Group protests, whether in the form of sporadic insurrection or of active or passive disobedience, are dealt with more or less severely according as the State considers them a real or a potential threat to its security. What also helps to decide the more or the less, in other words, the degree of disobedience that a State is prepared to tolerate or to turn a blind eye to, is the value which the majority attaches to the right of the minority to protest. And the decision of the majority will unquestionably be affected by the attitude taken by the minority in making its protest. In more concrete terms, the more safety-valves a constitution provides for the expression of minority opinions, the more they are likely to be used with discretion by minorities, and the more a minority shows itself conscious of the right of the majority to rule, the less reluctant that majority will be to make adequate provision for the expression of minority opinion.

What this pragmatic approach assumes is that both sides really want to make the system work. On this assumption, the majority makes concessions to the minority in recognition of their fundamental equality as individuals, and the minority respects the limits of the concession in recognition of the principle that the will of the majority ought to prevail. The result is one of four developments. Either the minority remains so small that some infraction of constitutional rules can be permitted, or winked at, without creating any further problems, or the majority ends by being convinced of the rightness of the minority case and changes its policy accordingly. The suffragette movement is perhaps an example of this second development. Or, alternatively, the minority movement finally loses its appeal and disappears, or it finds some constitutional form of activity. The assumption throughout is that, in so far as a challenge to the State exists, it does so on specific issues and does not weaken the State's general authority. In these circumstances, indeed, freedom to protest may very well strengthen the State's authority. For a State in which the citizen, whether he is in the majority or in the minority, is confident that he is valued as a human being has a degree of moral authority that may well prove unchallengeable.

The situation is quite different, however, where the minority objects to the whole purpose of the State, as expressed through the will of the majority, and where its object in disobeying the State is not to gain any particular end, but to overthrow the State itself. In other words, the democratic compromise solves nothing except when both sides care more in the last resort for the maintenance of democracy than for the assertion of their rights as a majority or a minority. What ought to be the attitude of a democratic State when it is confronted by a minority which rejects the principle of government by consent? How is it possible in these circumstances for it to save its soul without sacrificing its body, and *vice versa*?

It must be admitted that this situation presents a democratic Government with a moral dilemma which is almost insoluble. For, by practising the tolerance towards dissenting views which the democratic conscience calls for, a democratic Government is scrupulously putting into the hands of its opponents weapons which they will use unscrupulously in order to destroy it. In saving its soul it is endangering its body, because the two sides do not recognize the same rules. When in 1950, Mr. Arthur Deakin, then Secretary of the Transport and General Workers' Union, called in exasperation for the banning of the Communist party, he was not objecting to the right of any British citizen to believe in the Communist way of life. He was objecting to the specific activities of a minority of Communist Trade Unionists. In his view, these men did not believe in democracy, yet they were claiming, and profiting from, the freedom of action that they enjoyed by virtue of their citizenship in a democracy, in order to try to undermine the system itself. Mr. Deakin was, in effect, applying to the

Trade Union field the argument which Lord Balfour applied in 1927 to the political field when he doubted whether the British system would be able to deal with "violent situations". On this thesis, our political machinery presupposes a fundamental agreement about the way in which it is to be used. If one side refuses to stick to the rules, either that side must be prevented from abusing its rights by having the freedom to use them withdrawn, or the whole system will be endangered.

The questions which we have to answer as citizens of a democracy are these: How far is a democratic State justified in withdrawing democratic rights from those who consistently abuse them? If it has the right to do so, at what point ought it to take action? If the fact of abuse is proved to the satisfaction of some such body as a court of law, is that sufficient justification, or ought the Government to wait until the abuse constitutes a clear and actual threat to the State's security? How do we judge when that point has been reached, and, perhaps more important, who is to judge? Harold Laski argued that the citizen in a democracy ought to have the right to propagate revolution, but not to practise it. He believed that the individual could feel satisfied that he counted in the State, only if he were able to express himself freely, that individual liberty could not survive without freedom of the mind. "I can think," he said, "of no revolutionary period in history when a Government has gained by stifling the opinion of men who do not see eye to eye with it." But what if the opinions lead to action? Laski believed that when the revolutionary passes from theory to practice, the State has not merely the right but the duty to intervene, because "its duty to maintain peace and security lies at the very root of its existence. The liberty which associations enjoy must therefore be set in the context that they cannot have a liberty to overthrow the State." We judge that the danger point has been reached when the Government can "prove the commission of some overt act which directly tends to imminent rebellion."

This argument seems to leave out of account the possibility

of a long period of "cold war", during which political revolutionaries might use their legitimate freedom of action to
undermine their adversaries in advance, so that, by the time
they resorted to demonstrably illegitimate acts, the battle
might well have been virtually won. It is not easy to decide
where propaganda stops and "overt acts" begin. Incitements
to violence, the working up of widespread discontent or dis-
affection, may threaten the State just as seriously as an insurrection. It would have been quite possible for Mr. Deakin to
agree with his most ardent left-wing opponent on the general
definition of rights given by Harold Laski. But the two would
have differed irreconcilably in their interpretation of the
category in which the activity of Communist Trade Unionists
in 1950 ought to be placed.

Practical difficulties of interpretation of this kind have led
other thinkers to argue, as MacIver does, that "if men are not
content to win their ends by making enough converts to turn
their cause into the cause of the majority, so that it can legitimately triumph at the polls, they are rejecting the only ground
on which, in a democracy, they are entitled to ask for the
liberty of their opinions. They want to resort to violence—if
necessary—against the opinions of the majority, and they
have the effrontery to ask that democracy permit them to
marshal their forces to this end." The French philosopher,
Julien Benda, who had seen how toleration by pre-war French
Governments of the Fascist para-military groups helped to
undermine parliamentary republicanism and prepared the
way for the anti-democratic Government of Vichy France,
wrote during the temporary eclipse of democracy in France:
"We even recognize the right of democracy to take the initiative against an adversary who seeks to destroy democracy,
even if the adversary acts in such a way (as he invariably will)
that the intention cannot be definitely proved."[1]

This conclusion goes too far in the other direction. It seems

---

[1] *La Grande Epreuve des Démocraties* (Editions du Sagittaire, 1945), p. 131.

even more difficult to draw the line between legitimate and illegitimate intentions than between legitimate propaganda and "overt acts" threatening the overthrow of the State. If Laski's solution leaves the State without adequate means of defence against a fifth column, Benda's would appear to leave the citizen without adequate redress, if a Government were to decide arbitrarily that his intentions were not to criticize but to destroy. If Great Britain leans towards the first and France towards the second alternative, it may be, as Benda suggests, that English Governments have, so far, been able to take the risk—to permit themselves the luxury, as he puts it— only because British potential revolutionaries have not been strong enough to constitute a serious threat to democracy. France learnt by bitter experience in 1940 that a Fascist fifth column could betray democracy. In 1951, with over five million electors who continued to vote Communist, she was afraid that a Communist fifth column might, as the Communist leader, Maurice Thorez, suggested, in a speech in the Assembly in February 1949, refuse to defend France if her territory were invaded by Soviet Russia. The dilemma confronting the modern citizen is therefore by no means academic or remote. It could happen here. The point at which our country draws the line, whether we adopt protective defence measures along the lines advocated by Benda, with the risk that they may lead to restrictions on our freedom of opinion or action, perhaps to a banning of the Communist party, or whether we adopt the liberal interpretation of minority rights advocated by Laski, with the risk that we may have to win back by years of war the freedom jeopardized by that minority's abuse of democratic rights, or whether we reach some compromise between the two, will be determined, in a democracy, by the choice of the majority of the citizens. The least we can do, therefore, is to know what we choose and why.

We can, in all probability, do much more. For if there is no theoretically satisfactory solution, once the revolutionary minority is actually at work, there is much that can be done

7

at an earlier stage to prevent the situation from ever reaching that point. Indeed, it is possible to urge that the extent to which such a threat to the State exists is a measure of the success or failure of that system. For the wider the area of consent, the less will be the appeal of revolutionary doctrines. There is no need to preach violence when alternative methods exist. It is usually only when people despair of ever making their voices heard in any other way that they are prepared to pay the heavy price which a revolution inevitably entails. We have said earlier in this chapter that one of the strongest practical arguments against the revolutionary method is its unpredictability, the high risk that it entails that the revolutionary short cut may prove to be the longest way home. Clearly, few who were aware of it would be prepared to run such a risk if they had a reasonable hope of getting what they wanted, perhaps more slowly, but certainly more surely, by other means. A democracy which wishes to prevent the growth of revolutionary forces will, therefore, do everything in its power to allow for the peaceful evolution of institutions. Aristotle gave this piece of advice to the world over two thousand years ago, but it is still just as valid to-day. He held that revolutions were more likely to occur in an oligarchy than in a democracy, that is, when the few governed the many. "The wider the foundation," he said, "the securer the building and it is ever best to live where equality prevails."[1]

It must be pointed out here that the Marxist conception of history is one that rules out this solution. It denies the possibility of peaceful change because it denies the central assumption of democracy, namely, that society is made up of a multiplicity of conflicting wills of fundamentally equal individuals and groups. It starts from the assumption that what produces social change is conflict—at the present time, conflict between two social classes, rich and poor, exploiters and exploited,

---

[1] *Politics*, 1307a.

capitalists and workers, and that this conflict is so deep-rooted that it can be resolved only by unleashing the explosive forces of revolution. Now political science cannot *prove* that one of these assumptions, the Marxist and the democratic, is correct and the other incorrect. Neither can history. All that we can do is to look at the facts for ourselves and decide which particular set seems to us on the whole the more reasonable. But it is essential to look at the facts from both sides, not merely at those chosen by one side to bolster up its case. In the last resort, our choice will probably be determined as much by our temperament, heredity and traditions as by the arguments, since the arguments cannot be conclusive. Only two major powers—China and the Soviet Union—have up to now established a Marxist Socialist system of government, and only one, the U.S.S.R., can reasonably claim that it is a permanent régime. The two are in profound disagreement, while the East-European Communist States are almost wholly dominated by the U.S.S.R There are a number of older democracies. In the modern sense, however, democracy is still a very recent phenomenon and there is as yet no guarantee that it will continue to develop along present lines. After all, universal suffrage, which is merely the necessary first step on the road to obtaining the maximum consent of citizens, has existed in Britain only since 1929, and Frenchwomen did not vote until 1945. Democratic systems can still differ on almost every democratic institution—on electoral systems, on who should vote and when, and on the role of Parliaments and parties. The economic implications of democracy are more recent conceptions still. Whether we come down on the side of democracy, then, or of Marxist revolutionary theory, we shall necessarily be making an assumption, whose accuracy remains to be established by future generations. Even then, when the Marxist and democratic experiments of our time have become part of the history learnt by our descendants, the final answer will not have been given. For future generations are not likely to find it any easier than we do to read the lessons of history.

Democratic and Marxist theories have changed in response to changing circumstances and will no doubt continue to change. For instance, the Marxist view that the passage to Socialism must necessarily be revolutionary has been for some time now under increasing challenge, especially in European Communist parties. There are wide differences in democratic States regarding what ought to be the relationships between Parliaments and citizens, the scope and methods of State intervention in economic life, and the kind of institutions required to meet social demands in the conditions of a modern democracy. We have to find suitable institutions through which the millions of citizens in a contemporary democratic community can make their wishes felt and their opinion known. We have to educate them so that they understand the implications of the consent for which they are being asked, to make them interested in the problems of government, which touch their lives so closely, and ready to give up the time and energy required to participate intelligently in the conduct of affairs. If we fail in that task, there is always the danger that some political leader will be able to win support for a short cut, in the form of a Fascist or a Communist State, in which the citizen will be required to obey, but will not be expected—indeed will not be allowed—to undertake the hard responsibilities of self-government which democracy expects of him.

To try to indicate in any detail the kind of institutions we need to build a secure and responsible democracy would require another book.[1] All that can be done here is to suggest briefly the ways in which democracies have sought to solve these problems and what in some of them is being advocated for the future. Perhaps the most startling changes in the last century have been the broadening of the basis of representation and the levelling up of educational facilities. In 1832, immediately after the passage of the first Reform Bill,

---

[1]*See* Pickles, *Democracy* (Methuen, 1971).

the members of the House of Commons comprised 508 land-owners, 73 financiers and 100 professional soldiers or sailors. Up to 1924, only two sons of working men had achieved Cabinet rank, and up to 1906, over half of the Cabinet members, on an average, belonged to the aristocracy. Before 1882, only one member in forty of the population had the right to vote, and up to 1872 the right to vote by no means necessarily implied the right to vote as the elector wished, without incurring the risk of victimization. In 1851, out of a total of five million British children between the ages of three and fifteen, less than half were having any regular schooling. Only half of those who attended school remained until the age of eleven and only just over a quarter up to the age of thirteen. In 1869, education was still not compulsory and less than half of the working-class children were even on the registers of the Government-aided schools that then existed. Not until 1918 was free education up to the age of fourteen made compulsory, while nation-wide free secondary education dates only from 1944. From 1848, there was a slow and continuous development of health services. In 1911, some ten million insured workers were eligible for insurance against ill-health, but the system was not extended to the whole working population and made also available to the families of the insured workers until the introduction in 1948 of a comprehensive national system of insurance against unemployment, ill-health, widowhood and old age. All this process of intellectual and physical levelling up has been accompanied by a consistent widening of the field from which political and administrative rulers are chosen. In 1929, the whole adult population became electors, and in subsequent elections more than three-quarters of them exercised their right to vote. With the subsequent raising of the school-leaving age and lowering of the voting age, and with the expansion of University education in Western Europe in the 1960's and 1970's, the principles of equality of political rights and economic opportunities came to be more and more generally taken as matters of course. A man or woman of working-class origin is now no novelty in the Civil Service or the Cabinet.

These are great changes, and they have no doubt done much to increase the opportunities offered to citizens to feel that they are part of the State and have a hand in its running. But it is reasonable to ask oneself if they go far enough to widen the area of consent, in the way we have suggested as the most probable solution of the problem of change. There are only 635 members of the British Parliament, and so very few of the forty million British electors can hope to be elected. Even if we include local government representatives, the number of citizens who are able to share directly in the running of the country is bound to remain a very small minority indeed. What is there for the others? Is the area of consent wide enough to satisfy most people if they are asked every five years or so to put a cross against the name of a candidate about whom they usually know very little and of whose policy they may have only the haziest of ideas?

It is clear that attachment to a political party is not enough. Fewer than one in ten of those who vote for a party are prepared to become members, and fewer still to work for it actively. What techniques are needed to provide adequate opportunities to the other nine to feel themselves a vital part of the State in which they live and not a disgruntled minority, for whom the alternatives are passive dissatisfaction or active revolt?

A number of modern thinkers have sought the answer to this question, and three of the answers, at least, require consideration at this stage. The first believes that modern government is bound to be increasingly a matter for experts. Subjects like agricultural production, atomic research, the organization of the armed forces, the conditions of international trade, the housing target and thousands of others, afford the average citizen, or even the average Member of Parliament, little opportunity to make a real contribution. In *The Managerial Revolution*, an American author has argued that in modern societies the real rulers are the technicians and that, if Capitalism is doomed to disappear, it is not likely to be followed by Socialism, but rather by some form of government by experts. H. G. Wells, in his later years, attributed to experts, and particularly to those actually in control of industry, a predominant rôle in the process of social transformation. There was more than a streak of this "technocratic" approach in the thinking of Sydney and Beatrice Webb, although they envisaged the government of experts as, in the main, the government of civil servants. It was the Webbs who referred to the modern processes of government as "the work of an able and honest but secretive bureaucracy, tempered by the ever-present apprehension of the revolt of powerful sectional interests, and mitigated by the spasmodic interventions of imperfectly comprehending ministers."[1] The complexity of administration in large urban areas, the spread of delegated legislation, the increasing importance of scientists and technicians all tend to make government more and more a matter for the expert.

The second approach, with which the Webbs are more definitely associated, is a functional one. It attempts to reconcile the democratic principle with the facts of modern scientific and technological development, by bringing the citizen into the process of government on his own specialist level, as well as in his capacity as an elector. Each individual is something of a specialist at least in the field in which he works. And, what is perhaps more important, it is at the point at which his own life comes into contact with the State's regulations that his interest in politics can be most easily aroused. Attempts to provide for some kind of functional political representation range from proposals for an industrial Second Chamber, advocated in 1920, by Sydney and Beatrice Webb[2], and proposals made nearly thirty years ago (1947) by Christopher Hollis, M.P., in his book, *Can Parliament Survive?* for a kind of functional Third Chamber, to plans for extending consultation

---

[1] *A Constitution for the Socialist Commonwealth of Great Britain* (Longmans, 1920), pp. 64-71.
[2] *Ibid.*

between workers and managements in factory and workshop and between Government departments and representative citizens, and for granting to the workers in an industry a direct share in the running of it.

There are a number of obstacles to the application of the principle of direct functional political representation. First, it would be very difficult, if not impossible, to weight the different interests in a way acceptable to all of them. Second, and more important, the very procedure of a legislative body would seem to defeat the end for which the functional body was created. For legislation is general. It deals, inevitably, with a mass of complex technical questions, on each of which only a minority would possess the functional *expertise* for which they were chosen. It is hard to see why a Bill to deal with, say, the railways, should be more discerningly dealt with by a body in which only a minority knew anything about railways, than by a body constituted like the present House of Commons. Members of Parliament are chosen on general party lines, but they could probably produce as many members with a specialized background, either on railways or on anything else, as a functional Chamber would be able to do. The difference is that recruitment of specialized capacity under the present territorial system is haphazard and not a mathematically weighted affair, which is what functional representation would try to make it. Third, an expert who is himself likely to be personally or professionally affected by contemplated legislation constitutes a vested interest. There is a danger that he will be an advocate rather than a trustee in the national interest, which is what a legislator is expected to be in a democracy.

It is problems such as these which have persuaded many people that the true functional contribution ought not to be legislative, but advisory, and that the place for it is in the workshop and the factory, as well as in political committees. They believe that political responsibility ought to remain where it is now, with the democratically elected representatives. The Communists, it is true, always emphasize the need for "workers' control." But in the countries in which they could apply the principle they take care to see that all managers are orthodox Communists.

The functional approach cuts across party lines. Liberal and some Conservative opinion favour it in the form of profit-sharing or co-partnership schemes. Similarly, there are both Conservatives and Socialists who have advocated direct functional representation. The Labour and Trade Union movements have always included Syndicalist elements, although these have played a much smaller part in Great Britain than in some other countries, particularly in France, Italy and Spain. But at any Trade Union Congress, from one to half a dozen Trade Union leaders will advocate the Syndicalist principle of industrial management by the workers. In France and Italy, Conservative and Fascist opinion flirted with the idea of Corporatism and both Italy and France tried to apply it, the first under Mussolini, the second during the Vichy régime. The Fifth French Republic has an advisory functional Assembly and, since the war, Federal Germany has had a compulsory system of workers' participation in management.

Orthodox Socialist opinion, and much non-Socialist pro-gressive opinion, too, has always regarded much more favour-ably, however, the third approach to social change and to the problem of the citizen's participation in the processes of government. This is the gradualist, or, in its British Socialist form, the Fabian approach. Both believe that the expert, although essential, must continue to be responsible to and directed by the elected democratic representatives. The Fabians see in the State the chief initiator of social change. But they are conscious of the need for perpetual reformulation of the institutional implications of social changes and also of the need to devise machinery which can utilize adequately, not only the service of the expert, but also those of the citizen, whether in his functional capacity or in his capacity as a con-

sumer. The Fabians appeal directly to a small intellectual
and mainly academic *élite*. They are interested primarily
in the problem of techniques, in the adaptation of institutions
to changing human needs and to changing economic conditions. But their influence goes far beyond the Socialist and
left-wing, or progressive, circles to which they address themselves directly. In Great Britain, the ordinary intelligent
citizen, with his long tradition of local independence, his
strong sense of social responsibility and his belief in voluntary
social service, has more or less unconsciously grafted on to the
Christian and Liberal reformism of the nineteenth century
a certain amount of Fabianism, if not in the form of acceptance
of Fabian doctrine, at least in the form of acceptance of much
of the Fabian approach.

Indeed, all three approaches are perceptible in the modern
British attitude to social change. The average citizen, whether
he approves of planning in principle or not, tends to conceive of
it in practice less in bureaucratic terms than did the early
Fabians. He thinks of it not so much as State control as of
expert management under the general supervision of the
State. Whether in services such as education and public
health, in nationalized industries such as the Post Office,
British Rail, gas, electricity and the mines, in large and
to some degree autonomous corporations such as the B.B.C., or
in large private concerns such as I.C.I., Unilever or the car
industry, or in the very many hybrid institutions that exist in
Britain today, management is though of essentially as a
job for experts enjoying a generous degree of freedom to
try out technical experiments. In practice, all parties are
committed to some degree of Government intervention, or
planning, though they do not agree either on the circumstances
in which or on the extent to which Governments should seek
to guide or control economic development.

The citizen has, too, something of the functional approach.
It is clear that there is a general belief in the desirability and
possibility of co-operation between Government departments

and experts and between Government departments and industrial or professional associations, such as the National Farmers' Union, the Press Association, the British Medical Association, to quote only one or two. Whatever views members of these or other associations may hold as to the wisdom or unwisdom of the policy a particular Government is pursuing at any particular time, they still claim the right to be consulted, to negotiate and, as far as possible, to co-operate with Government departments. It is significant that throughout the war the British press accepted censorship voluntarily and built up a co-operative relationship, instead of doing as the French press did and appearing day after day with blank spaces where articles had been cut out by the censorship. It seems reasonably certain, however, that most British citizens would not like to see the functional principle extended, either in the direction of right-wing Corporatism, or of left-wing Syndicalism. The average citizen clings firmly to the principle of the final responsibility of the directly elected political representatives.

He believes passionately, too, in the need to provide for individual initiative and local diversities. And because he is traditionally conditioned to think of social change in institutional rather than in doctrinal and theoretical terms, he tends to have a pragmatic approach and to ask himself how this or that will work, or whether it will work, rather than what ought, in principle, to work, and to try to make it work by tentative and gradual experiments before committing himself to sweeping changes in principle. For social change, whether peaceful or revolutionary, cannot be divorced from the background of history and custom, tradition and national prejudice, which, as we have seen, determine the way in which we look at all political problems. Marxists regard their theories as capable of international application, precisely because they deny the validity of this background, though whether even they are able in practice to ignore it is another matter. But democratic change, whether it comes by revolution or by evolution, must take men's background into account all the time. However violent a break is made with the past, the democratic method, in Great Britain at least, is to make that break gradually, by modifying and building on foundations that are already there. Whether this approach will enable the British system to meet the challenge of the new social forces that have come to the fore in the twentieth century, and to do so without either revolutionary upheaval or political deadlock and frustration, whether British citizens will be able to steer a middle course between the dangers of revolution and "the dangers of obedience", is a question that only the future can answer.

CHAPTER FIVE

The State in Relation to Other States

IN all that has been said up to now regarding the relations between the State and the citizen, we have been arguing as if nations lived in total isolation. No account has been taken of the impact of other States on either Government or citizens. In the twentieth century, this is certainly a totally unrealistic assumption. If one State is in conflict with another, or if conflict is threatened, then a State's freedom of action may be severely curtailed and many of the problems that have been discussed in earlier chapters will take on different aspects. The rights of minorities to protest against the Government's policy, the rights of groups to foster attachments to bodies other than the State, or even to other States, cannot, as we have seen, be determined absolutely. A State which is fighting, or fears that it may have to fight, for survival, is likely to view the claims of such groups or minorities quite differently from the way a strong and peaceful community will look on them. If the nations of the world cannot eliminate the threat of war, at least to the extent to which nation-States have succeeded in eliminating the danger of civil war, then the sense of national insecurity will be bound to hamper, if it does not prevent, the normal democratic processes of political and social evolution.

Men have been trying for centuries to find some international organ, or some system of international law, capable of preventing nations from resorting to war to settle their disputes. Yet, near the end of the twentieth century, and after two world wars within a generation, there is still no certainty in the world regarding the possibility of preventing aggression. The United Nations, which represents the most recent of a long series of attempts to deal with the problem, is still no more than a voluntary association of sovereign States. It has no power to compel a State to surrender any of its national sovereign rights. In the last resort, there is no means by which a recalcitrant member can be forced to comply with the rules that the United Nations have laid down. The first real test of the United Nations' ability to defend the new internationalism against aggression came in June 1950, just five years after its foundation, when South Korea was attacked by North Korea. It cannot be said that this provided a convincing demonstration of the ability of the United Nations to compel respect for the provisions of the Charter, and succeeding tests—in the Middle East, in 1956, and in the Congo in 1960—were even less encouraging. There is still no real guarantee against aggression, except the power of the victim to retaliate. What the nations of the world are faced with is the need to make international institutions work positively so that aggression may become not only unprofitable, but unthinkable. There is a long and difficult road ahead of them before that point is likely to be reached.

In every century, going back to the Middle Ages, there have been men who have tried to find ways of preventing war. Before the nation-State as we know it came into being, the solution was generally envisaged in terms of religious unity, through an extension of the influence or authority of the Pope. With the development of the nation-State and the growth of Protestantism, the Catholic Church ceased to be either a sufficiently strong or a sufficiently unifying force on which to base an international organization. In the sixteenth and seventeenth centuries, while writers or preachers might pay lip-service to peace and denounce war as cruel and evil, the rulers of European States were bound by no rules that they did not choose to accept. The only check on national aggressiveness was the fear of being defeated. Monarchs protected themselves by alliances or used alliances as instruments of aggression. The eighteenth-century writer, Montesquieu, said that absolute monarchy and international law were incompatible and certainly they proved to be so in practice.

In 1625, the Dutch lawyer, Grotius, often described as the father of international law, published a treatise on *The Laws of Peace and War*. Three quarters of it is taken up with attempts to lay down some rules for the conduct of war, in order to mitigate to some extent its cruelty and barbarity. When it came to suggesting ways of preventing war, he had little to say beyond expressing the general conviction that Christian kings and Christian States were specially called upon to arbitrate, if by so doing they could avoid war. "For this reason," he says, "as for others, it would be useful, and we may say necessary, that conferences should be established between the Christian Powers to settle disputes by the voice of those nations who are not themselves affected by the controversy in question."[1] He saw that some method of compelling the parties to accept the verdict would have to be found, but had no proposals to offer on this vital point. The founder of the American Quaker movement, William Penn, proposed the setting up of an International Parliament to "establish rules of justice for sovereign princes to observe one to another." He went even farther and urged that nations refusing to submit disputes to this body or to abide by its decisions should be compelled, by the combined force of the others, both to submit and to pay damages to any injured nation.

William Penn was one of the few thinkers of this period who looked at the problem in a practical way. Most of the pacifists of the seventeenth and eighteenth centuries—and this age produced a host of pacific sentiments and schemes for international peace—looked at the problem in one of two ways. Either they assumed that men would ultimately have the sense to give up making war because it was clearly wrong and unjust,

---

[1] Quoted in F. Melian Stawell's, *The Growth of International Thought*, pp. 122-3 (Home University Library, 1929).

or else they assumed that they would do so because it was demonstrably unprofitable. Their hopes lay in "the progress of universal reason". As Kant put it: "Nature will drive them with the scourge of war, with the extravagant and ever-growing burden of armaments, the weight of which must be felt in the end by every State even when at peace. She will compel them to make attempts, halting at first and incomplete, and then, after much desolation, destruction and revolution, to do what reason could have taught them at once without so many bitter experiences, namely, to give up their lawless life of savages and enter into a League of Nations—an organization where every State—even the smallest, can expect security and peace, not from its own power or its own decision as to what is right in its own cause, but from this great Society of Nations . . . where the powers of all are united in one and the decision is given by the general will acting according to law."[1] Montesquieu argued that, with the growth of commerce, nations were becoming more and more interdependent and that the havoc wrought by war harmed victors as well as vanquished. Armaments led to an armament race and "nothing is gained but common ruin". It was still possible at this time to assume that justice and right were both discoverable and recognizable and that once men were able to see the light of reason, they would accept its dictates as their rule of conduct.

The nineteenth century was an age of dominant nationalism. If men thought more in terms of institutions and less in terms of the progress of reason, the institutions which they devised to preserve peace were still no more than alliances between independent and often rival nations. The machinery was bound, therefore, to remain consultative. It was not until the turn of the century that the first decisive steps were taken along the road which was to lead in fifty years to two attempts to establish a world organization to preserve peace. In 1907, as a result of the Hague Peace Conference, a Permanent Tribunal

---

[1] *Ibid.* pp. 198-9.

was set up to deal with international disputes. Its scope was limited, however, to disputes susceptible of a legal settlement. It could neither compel a nation to submit a dispute to arbitration, nor enforce its decision when a dispute was submitted. War came in 1914, and with it came the realization that something far more comprehensive was needed if wars were to be prevented in the future. One of the most important tasks of the Peace Conference which followed that war was, therefore, the creation of the League of Nations. Ten years after its foundation, the League had already proved itself a sad disappointment to those who had hoped that it would be able to provide some real protection against war. It did, in fact, help to settle pacifically a number of disputes. But its authority was never accepted unquestioningly and its decisions were in effect applicable only when no interests of a Great Power were vitally involved. By 1935, it was clear that, in the event of a clash between major Powers, it would be totally unable to prevent them from going to war to settle it.

The League never succeeded in overcoming three fundamental weaknesses. First, it never discovered a satisfactory method of reaching its decisions. In theory, all League members, being sovereign States, were equal. In practice, of course, they were not. If they had really been equal, it might have been possible, or at least logical, to decide issues by majority vote. The facts of the world situation ruled this out. It would have given a combination of small nations the power to dominate the League Assembly, although the Great Powers constituted half the total world population. To weight the vote, on a population basis, however, would have been no more realistic, for it would have given to politically inexperienced and militarily backward countries, like India or China, a power out of all proportion to their real influence in the world at that time. In an effort to get away from power politics, the League Covenant ignored the real implications of power, namely the inescapable responsibility of the Great Powers for preserving peace, since they alone were in a position to fight a major war. The real danger of war lay in the risk of a clash between one or other of half a dozen powerful members of the League or between one or other of them and a powerful State outside it. The first requisite of peace was, therefore, agreement between the Great Powers, and decisions reached in any way which failed to take account of this were bound to be irrelevant or ineffective.

What the League did was to try to compromise between the theoretical ideal of equality and the practical recognition that it did not exist. The Covenant safeguarded the fiction of equality by requiring all decisions to be unanimous, thus condemning itself from the start to advance only at the pace of the slowest. Inequality was recognized by the provision that certain countries should be permanent members of the Council, upon which the real responsibility for leadership and decision devolved.

When the United Nations was created in 1945, the founders tried not to repeat the mistake of requiring unanimous decisions. They replaced the general right of veto by the right of veto of the Great Powers who were permanent members of the Security Council. They did so because it was generally realized that the effective power to safeguard peace belonged to the "big five". The device rapidly produced total deadlock, however, because no international organization has yet succeeded in solving the second of the problems, which is the essential weakness of international government, its inherent inability to deal with a situation in which power is divided equally—or so nearly equally as to make it impossible for one side to impose its will on the other—between nations, or groups of nations, which differ on issues so fundamental as to make compromise virtually impossible.

We have already seen that national government, if it is to function effectively, assumes a certain homogeneity of opinion, at least on the methods, if not on the purposes of government. No system of government can work unless a sufficient number of people are prepared to abide by a minimum number of rules of political behaviour. Among these rules, one of the most essential is the renunciation of force as a method of gaining political ends. The same argument applies to the government of an international community. If powerful elements of an international association break away and attack others, then the whole organization breaks down. It cannot function effectively, where there is even a threat of such action. Whether national or international, government assumes that a majority of the governed will try to make the system work and that disobedience will occur only as an isolated phenomenon and will not be such as to threaten the authority of the association itself. Nothing either in the League of Nations Covenant or in the Charter of the United Nations could conceivably guarantee the preservation of peace, once a powerful enough group of nations was bent on destroying it.

The League was unable to harmonize national interests sufficiently to prevent such a situation from arising. When it did, the offender simply contracted out of the organization, thus leaving national interests with a free hand. In the United Nations, cynicism has gone a step farther. The offender can remain a member and use the veto to prevent the organization from exercising any real control over national policy.

The third major weakness of international government is the lack of efficient methods of enforcing decisions, even assuming agreement can be reached. The nations which contracted out in the 'thirties—Spain, Italy and Germany—were far less powerful than Russsia and her satellites are to-day. But the League possessed no organ by which an offender could be brought speedily to reason. A nation-State, as we have seen, can enforce obedience, if necessary, by resorting to the use of armed force against offenders. The League had no International Army. It had not even an International Police Force. It was not a super-State but an association of sovereign States, each of which retained control of its own police and its own defence forces. There was no machinery which would enable these national units to combine quickly and effectively so as to constitute an international force to uphold the authority of the League. It is true that if the members of the Council had wanted to act they could have made more effective use of the existing machinery and could easily have made it more efficient. The real weakness was in the men. Nations were not in agreement and they did not want to abandon their national sovereignty. Indeed, during the inter-war years, the conception of the League as a kind of super-State, with some specified degree of sovereignty over member States, was one which the Great Powers categorically rejected. Nothing that the League did, nothing that it had the theoretical power to do, involved the abandonment by any of its members of a single claim to national sovereignty.

Of course, any international agreement carries with it the acceptance of some limitation on independent national action. But the limitations are specific; they are in the nature of a temporary suspension of sovereignty, voluntarily agreed to. They do not constitute a permanent relinquishment of sovereignty. League commitments were never more than international agreements between sovereign States. They differed from other international agreements, not in form, but in intention, in scope, and in the expressed will to go farther as circumstances permitted. In 1932, the French Government proposed the creation of an International Army. The proposal was turned down. The Charter of the United Nations did endeavour to give the organization the "teeth" that the League had lacked by providing for the creation of an international force. But the military committee to which this task was to be entrusted never achieved anything, because the Russians refused to attend. In 1950, when disappointment at the failure of the United Nations to make any appreciable progress towards real international control had led the European nations to turn to regional organizations, such as the Council of Europe and Western European Union, France proposed the creation of a European army constituted by the six member-nations of the Coal–Steel Pool. For four years, the six would-be partners were unable to agree sufficiently on the conditions in which they would feel safe in replacing their national defence forces by a supra-national force—the European Defence Community—and eventually the project was abandoned. Confidence in the stability of international institutions has never been great enough for nations to feel convinced that the units of such an army, faced with a conflict between national and international loyalties, would not find the former stronger than the latter. Without that confidence, there would be small chance of solving the difficult technical problems that the existence of an international army would create—problems, for example, concerning the size of the different national contingents, the points at which they ought to be stationed, the nature of the arms with which they ought to be provided and the shares of different nations in that provision, the methods by which the international forces should be called into action and the occasions on which they ought to be used.

The fact is that, although in the long run it is both politically and economically in the interests of individual nations to act in concert, there may often be a very real conflict between national short-run and long-run interests. Indeed, it is sometimes almost impossible for a nation to decide where one ends and the other begins. A Government can decide, as Hitler did, to ignore long-run implications and deliberately risk a world war, gambling on the chances of a quick victory which would bring material gains outweighing the losses caused by war. Or a nation can defy international opinion, as Russia did when she sent troops into Hungary in 1956 and in 1968 into Czechoslovakia, sure in the knowledge that no great Power is likely to risk launching a major war (nowadays almost certainly a nuclear war) in order to defeat a minor, non-nuclear, aggression. Or again, nations can decide, as France and Great Britain did, at the same time as the Russian invasion of Hungary, that the impotence of the United Nations to prevent threats to peace in the Middle East justified them in taking action on their own, when Israel attacked Egypt in order to forestall an expected Egyptian attack.

It would be a mistake, however, to assume that no progress has been made. United Nations attitudes are not wholly without impact on Governments (as was seen in the Arab-Israeli disputes in the 1960's and 1970's). They can sometimes help to strengthen existing public opinion. And it was public opinion that led to trouble in every European Communist Party following the suppression of the Hungarian and Czech risings.

In France, for instance, which had the strongest Communist party in Europe, prominent left-wing intellectuals, formerly sympathetic to Communism, openly expressed their criticisms and there were a number of resignations from the French Communist party. The Suez incident, on the other hand, failed to achieve its aim, because Great Britain decided that she could not continue to defy the condemnations of her action in the United Nations, particularly by members of the Commonwealth. The United Nations took over the task of freeing traffic in the Suez Canal, and contingents supplied by members of the United Nations policed parts of the frontier between the two countries. When fighting broke out in 1961 in Tunisia, between Tunisians and French troops occupying the French naval base at Bizerta, Tunisia appealed to the Security Council which ordered both sides to cease hostilities and withdraw their troops. The order was obeyed. In 1960, when fighting in the Congo was threatening to become a danger to peace in Africa, an international force under United Nations command undertook to try to restore peace and order. When fighting broke out at the end of 1963 between Greek and Turkish Cypriots, British troops were at first sent in to try to keep peace between the two sides, but very shortly the United Nations took over the task.

None of these examples necessarily brought the constitution of an effective international army significantly nearer. But at least they revealed an evolution of opinion, and the beginnings of the development of something like an international conscience.

It can be argued, of course, that, in the nuclear age, no power could prevent a nuclear war from being started by one of the two great nuclear powers. In 1962, the Cuba affair showed how suddenly such a threat could develop, and how completely the peace of the world was in the hands of the United States and the Soviet Union. For some, the main hope lies in the restriction of nuclear weapons to these two Powers, and in the maintenance of "a balance of terror" until such time as it is possible for them to agree to negotiated nuclear disarmament by stages. Others, and notably France under the

Gaullist régime, have seen peace as being, at least in theory, better preserved by strengthening European institutions, including defence, while these continue to rely in practice on defence by the U.S.A. and NATO. But whether or not the finger on the nuclear trigger remains limited to the rulers of the two major nuclear Powers, there are many people both in France and Britain who believe that these two countries ought to play at least a minor nuclear role in order to prevent them from being no more than satellites of America in the field of defence. Others, on the contrary, believe that any spread of nuclear weapons involves more dangers than safeguards.

It seems then that, in the search for a rational constitutional relationship between nation-States, the fundamental obstacles to international organization are as difficult to surmount as ever they were. The international community remains no more than an ideal, because nations have never succeeded in building up sufficient confidence in international institutions to enable them to give up their national defence systems. But there have been advances on subordinate fronts. The growth of a sense of international solidarity has been marked during the course of the present century by the establishment, not merely of a vast network of inter-governmental bodies, but also of a series of international functional organizations and of a large number of voluntary international associations. To mention only a few at random, we have seen the formation of bodies like the League against Imperialism, the Inter-Parliamentary Union, the Pan-American Union, the Liberal International, Socialist, Trade-Union and Communist international organizations, the Women's International League, the International Students' Union. All these, and many others, bear witness to the growing realization that many of the problems that we have to deal with have their counterpart in other countries and that their solution is more rationally sought on international than on national lines. International conferences on subjects as far apart as Philately, an International language, and World Government have become accepted and normal events. Even in the nineteenth century, international non-political technical bodies existed whose decisions could bind national States (within certain limited spheres) without their specific consent. The Universal Postal Union, for example, goes back to 1874, the International Telegraphic Union even farther. But if we look for a moment only at the international organizations that grew up under the aegis of the League of Nations and that have already been formed under that of the United Nations, it is clear that they cover an enormous field of human activity, technical and scientific as well as political and economic. The League had committees to deal with economic and commercial relations, committees on the standardization of statistics, committees of information, for economic research into such problems as the trade cycle and fluctuations in the purchasing power of gold, committees to study the possibilities of international intellectual co-operation, to study agricultural problems, communications—including such subjects as free transit, passports, international railway traffic, the internationalization of motorists' and maritime signals. There were committees on social and humanitarian subjects—on health, child welfare, the drug traffic, the traffic in women and children, refugees and slavery. The International Labour Office constituted an independent organization dealing with the complex problems of labour relations and conditions. To-day, many international technical bodies have been incorporated in one or other of the dozen or so specialized agencies set up within the framework of the United Nations. The problems of post-war recovery stimulated the growth of a whole series of new organs of international co-operation. Within the framework of Europe, the Organization for European Co-operation and Development, Benelux, the Council of Europe, the Coal–Steel Pool, and the European Economic Community were set up to co-ordinate or integrate the different national policies. And the European Economic Community has repeatedly declared its intention of going on from economic to political integration, of creating some form of European—or more exactly west-European—union.

So complex and widespread has the network of international relations and international agencies now become that it is impossible for the average citizen of to-day to know anything about more than a small fraction of them. Yet, if he thinks about international problems at all, he is bound to ask himself at least two questions before he tries to decide what precisely is the value of all these international ramifications. He will want to know, first, whether they help to make war less likely than it would otherwise have been. Exactly what is their contribution towards a solution of the fundamental problem of international political anarchy? Does it in fact constitute a contribution, or are all these achievements liable to be swept away in a flash if war comes? His second question is: Where do we go from here? How he answers it will depend to some extent on the answer that he gives to the first question.

Both are difficult questions to answer. There are internationalists who sincerely believe that the surest road to a stable international organization of society is through the establishment of closer and closer functional links, along the lines that we have indicated. There are others who hold, no less sincerely, that, until the political foundations of the international community are securely laid, the functional edifice will be built only on sand. Whether carried on in association with, or independently of, the League, or the United Nations, these functional associations have undoubtedly done a great deal to introduce certain minimum standards throughout much of the civilized world. They have helped, too, to prepare people's minds to accept the principle of sharing out scarce goods on a basis of need, rather than on the basis of the ability of the powerful to grab. It was no mean achievement that, in the painful and difficult years immediately following the war, the European Coal Commission was able to share out the pitifully inadequate coal supplies on a more rational and just basis than would otherwise have been possible, and that, in spite of the great need that had to remain unmet, the nations of Europe agreed to ration themselves in the common interest. Similarly, Marshall Aid was shared out among the recipients on the basis of calculations arrived at by international negotiation and agreement. The Food and Agriculture Organization is tackling the problem of adjusting the world's food resources to world needs. The international planning of the years of post-war reconstruction represented a tremendous advance, not only on anything that was done in the years immediately following the first World War, but also on what was done during the whole of the inter-war period.

If and when international government comes into being, it will be all the more secure for being built on a foundation of practical co-operation. But are we any nearer to putting a date to the "if" and "when"? To recognize the value of the work done by functional associations is one thing; to assume that because it is valuable it must necessarily lead to closer political union is another. Indeed, it is arguable that the political obstacles to international government are even greater to-day than they were before all these functional developments took place. When the League of Nations was founded, Communism was the philosophy of an infant revolutionary State—and a delicate infant at that—whereas, to-day, it is the accepted political faith of a growing part of the world's population and the major source of international discord. If functional preparation is a necessary preparation for international government, it still does not follow that the essential step from the functional to the political plane can be taken except as a deliberate act of policy by national Governments. Nor is the argument from the facts of world interdependence any more conclusive. With the decolonization of almost the whole of Africa in the 'fifties and 'sixties of the twentieth century, the gulf between those who were in a position to supply technical and financial aid and those who depended on such aid to make political independence a reality grew more pronounced. The increasing birthrate added to the need for increased and co-ordinated aid by developed to under-developed countries. The difficulty is not so much to convince people of these facts, as to convince them that nations can find some workable method of dealing with the facts.

It has been clear to reflective citizens for centuries that the theory of isolated sovereign States bears little relation either to the economic or to the political facts. Governments have often had to fight hard in order to prevent the policy of one State from having what they considered to be undesirable repercussions on another. France's neighbours, and not least Great Britain, were actively concerned to prevent the spread to their own countries of the theories of the French Revolution. The Russian Communist experiment met with vigorous opposition —and even direct intervention—in its early years. To-day, all the evidence points to a desire on the part of Soviet Russia, at least for the time being, to find some *modus vivendi* with the West. But there is no sign that Communist China, Russia's rival for Communist domination in the emergent States of Africa and Asia, is as yet prepared for any similar, general understanding with the non-Communist world.

It may well be, indeed, that in spite of the facts of economic interdependence, countries with differing ideologies will find that these set a limit to the possibilities of international co-operation. Most of the newly independent States of Africa and Asia are Socialist or Socialistic, but, because they are so poor, they do not want to see the economic aid, on which their continued existence as independent States depends, restricted on political grounds. They are prepared to accept aid from both capitalist or Communist countries, provided no political strings are attached. For the most part, therefore, they have adopted a position of "non-alignment", refusing to commit themselves in international organizations to unquestioning support either of the Communist or the non-Communist *bloc*. But when political crises occur, it is not always possible to avoid taking sides. When Communist China attacked the North-Eastern frontier of India, it was not only India's traditional policy of non-alignment that was subjected to severe strains, but also that of like-minded countries. Similarly, when the Franco-Tunisian dispute broke out in 1961, the sympathies of the uncommitted nations were almost wholly on the side of

Tunisia, partly on the merits of the case, partly because the newly independent States are conscious of their special bonds as countries recently freed from colonial or quasi-colonial status.

Nor is it only ideological concepts such as anti-colonialism that can determine international sympathies, even at the cost of possible economic disadvantage. Among the more developed countries of western Europe, closer economic bonds have brought political friction. There is no doubt that the British Labour Government's hesitation to participate in the Coal–Steel Pool in 1950 was determined in part by the consciousness that two of the three great European steel-producing industries were in private hands, while the Labour Party, at that time, saw the future of British steel as a nationalized concern. There was also, in general, a fear among Labour supporters that an international body, such as the Coal–Steel Pool, might interfere with national policies. Similar fears existed at first when the European Economic Community came into being in 1957. Experience of the actual working of the EEC did much to dissipate these fears, so that when, in 1961, and again in 1967, Britain applied for membership, there were supporters and opponents in all British political parties.

This was not the only source of political friction, however. One difficulty that contributed to the failure of the first negotiations on British admission to the European Economic Community was the absence among the six members of the EEC of any kind of political relationship similar to that of Great Britain with other members of the Commonwealth. The British tended to take it for granted that the Six would make exceptions to meet British problems. The Six saw no reason either then or in 1970–71 to pay a higher price than necessary to assist either the British economy or British relations with the Commonwealth that meant nothing to them.

These are only a few examples of the obstacles that nations are bound to encounter as they extend the field of their co-operation. There is no hard and fast line between economics and politics. Indeed, political doctrines without economic and social implications would be arid and meaningless. It is, therefore, conceivable that, instead of functional co-operation between nations with differing political philosophies leading to closer political unity, we may find that lack of political unity sets a limit to functional co-operation. To admit this, however, does not necessarily imply that increasing international integration, whether economic or political, is impossible until nations can all agree with each other. It does suggest that philosophical or political differences between nations make international negotiation both more complex and more difficult and that, if they want to succeed in achieving a greater degree of international integration, nations will need all the tolerance and willingness to compromise that they are capable of. The practical experience of European co-operation is encouraging in that it does not suggest that ideological differences between countries with democratic, parliamentary Governments have so far constituted insuperable obstacles to closer international co-operation. It is discouraging in that it does suggest that the obstacles are much more difficult to surmount when it comes to world co-operation, where democratic and Communist-controlled countries would be required to work together.

Nowhere have these obstacles been more clearly perceptible than in the field of policy regarding under-developed countries. Communists hold that the necessary preliminary to economic advance is political revolution, that only under Communist direction can that advance be along the right lines. The democratic view is that political democracy can be built up only slowly on a basis of improved social and economic conditions, which will permit of education for democracy. The world has not yet found a generally accepted half-way house between these two conceptions, if, indeed, there is one to be found. To Stalin, the whole conception of a prolonged period of preparation for independence looked like badly camouflaged imperialism. Nor could the democracies prove by any immediately conclusive test that their intentions were not predatory. The age of economic imperialism is not so far distant that all fear of it is dead. The independence of virtually all the former colonial territories of Africa and Asia provides evidence of the sincerity of democratic motives, but to a Communist that evidence is far from conclusive, since political independence does not necessarily rule out the possibility of less visible, but perhaps no less effective, economic domination. To the democracies, the Communist approach is no less suspect. Nothing about the policy of Russia's satellites encourages outside observers to believe that they are anything but helpless tools of the Soviet Union. No evidence that filters out from behind the Iron Curtain convinces them that Soviet domination is increasing either their economic prosperity or their political freedom. On the contrary. The democracies believe, too, that Communist support for nationalist movements in under-developed countries, or for revolutionary opposition movements in young States is not inspired by genuine sympathy with the national aspirations of these territories, but is an instrument of Communist imperialism, inadequately camouflaged by the vocabulary of democratic Socialism.

The student who tries to make up his mind between these two ideologies is hampered, first, by the virtually insuperable difficulty of interpreting correctly the complex phenomena of modern international politics, and, second, by the practical impossibility of obtaining objective or complete evidence as to what is really going on behind the Iron Curtain. For the most part, he has to be content with glimpses, seen through the spectacles either of the Soviet Union's fanatical supporters or of its bitter opponents. Conscientious observers who try to provide him with dispassionate and factual accounts suffer to a greater or less degree from his own disabilities in that their opportunities for direct observation are extremely limited. In the last resort, the average student has to accept the word of one side or the other and try, even if inadequately, to judge for himself how far the facts of the international situation square with the expressed policies of the different Powers. The existence of the United Nations and the public discussion of disputed issues that takes place in the Assembly and the Security Council will at least give him some idea, not only of the attitudes of other countries to the policies of the two great *blocs*, but also of what each side is actually doing through the United Nations specialized agencies, to put internationalism into practice. He will rarely be able to verify for himself how far the case for either side, as presented to the United Nations, constitutes the whole truth, or even part of the truth, but he will be able to glean from the interchanges and the national alignments sufficient circumstantial evidence to help him to come down on one side or the other with some degree of confidence.

The answer to the second question, namely, what ought to be the next step on the road to internationalism, is bound up with the answer to the first. If, as our argument suggests, the nations of the world are becoming more and more interdependent, without any accompanying political *rapprochement*, then the inescapable implication is that functional co-operation, while it can help to strengthen the links between likeminded countries, can do little to avert the danger of a major clash between politically divergent *blocs*. It is no use arguing that if nations do not hang together they will end by hanging separately unless we can find acceptable ways in which they *can* hang together. How, then, are we to avoid war until such times as we can find a way of solving the major problem?

There have been four main answers to this question, together with a number of reserves, differences, and doubts regarding the methods by which, in each case, the principles could, or ought to be, put into operation. The first answer is that there can be no lasting solution to the problem of world peace without an easing of tension and some agreement between East and West. So far, it has seemed that this could happen only on Soviet terms, for the Soviet Union has steadfastly rejected all proposals for disarmament put forward by spokesmen of Western nations, while the latter have found it impossible to accept Soviet proposals. By August 1966, in spite of suggestions that the Soviet Union had had a change of heart, the 17-nation disarmament conference meeting at Geneva had held 286 plenary meetings without making any progress. By 1976, the figure had risen to well over 600.

There have been a number of differences regarding the methods by which East-West agreement should be sought. President de Gaulle, for instance, refused to have anything to do with the current disarmament discussions, since he regarded negotiations with the Soviet Union as useless, without more tangible evidence that the Russians meant business. The other seventeen nations believed that, with or without such assurances, it was always better to discuss than to refuse to discuss. Some have held that, since the main danger of nuclear war comes from the two major nuclear powers, there is more hope of a bi-lateral settlement than there is of agreement being reached between a dozen to twenty nations. The existence of the "hot line" between Moscow and Washington, and the speedy settlement of the Cuba crisis by America and Russia both provide some evidence to support this view. On the other hand, if by "peace" is understood, not merely the absence of war, but the organization of regular and accepted procedures for settling all disputes without resort to war, then a Russo-American agreement would not be enough to guarantee freedom from all war. The United Nations, as the only world-wide organization with the predominant aim of keeping the peace, and with all its specialized agencies seeking solutions for problems of poverty, disease and economic backwardness, would seem to be the natural organ for ensuring peace.

Unfortunately, recent developments seem to be making the United Nations less equipped to carry out such functions in proportion as the organization becomes more representative of the nations of the world. For with the admission of more and more of the former colonial territories as they become independent, while it is becoming more and more a forum—and a useful forum, as has already been pointed out—for the discussion of international problems, and sometimes for the exercise of pressure in support of certain actions, it is becoming less capable of taking the kind of decisive action that would be required in a major international crisis. It is divided into three main (and a number of subsidiary) groupings. There are, first the members, or supporters, of the Atlantic alliance. These include three of the five Great Powers, each of which can, by means of its veto, prevent any decision from being reached or any action from being taken which does not suit its own interests. There are, second, the members of the Soviet *bloc*, which is in a similar position of strength. The Soviet Union itself has had almost a monopoly of the right of veto. Indeed United Nations action in Korea was made possible only because the absence of the Russian delegate to the Security Council when the decision was taken prevented Russia from using the veto.

The largest group—which may soon constitute a majority in the General Assembly—is that of neutral and neutralist nations, the most numerous section being that of the Afro-Asian nations. None of these could implement any decision taken in the United Nations. They can supply token forces as indeed they have done on a number of occasions, but such forces can be effective only on condition that the countries in which such action is taken are themselves willing, at least in principle, to recognize United Nations authority. They could not supply even the puniest of armies to restrain one of the Great Powers from any action. Nor can the Great Powers be relied on to prevent—or even restrain—conflicts, either between or within smaller nations. The prospect following the decolonization of Portuguese African territories in 1975 and 1976 was one of more extensive and more dangerous African conflicts than earlier ones had been.

Nor is the veto the only method of rendering the United Nations powerless. While the formation of an international army is still as unlikely a prospect as it was in 1932, the United Nations is finding it more and more financially difficult to rely on voluntary national contingents. At the end of 1963, debts of nearly 150 million dollars were owing to the United Nations—95 millions on account of UN action in the Congo, 33 millions on account of action in the Middle East, and 19 millions owing to the non-payment by certain members of their regular contributions. The USSR, France, Nationalist China and the Congo refused to pay anything towards the Congo action; the USSR and Nationalist China refused to contribute to UN action in the Middle East and these two, together with Argentina, were in arrears with their normal contributions. The Soviet Union alone had accumulated a debt of 58 million dollars. Far from extending the scope of its action, the United Nations seemed likely to see even its normal activities brought to a standstill for financial reasons. Since then, political deadlocks have further reduced its effectiveness.

The second and third answers provided to the question as to how the nations of the world could keep the peace in the existing state of world opinion cannot really be regarded as practical politics. That of most of the neutrals and Afro-Asian neutralists is really to contract out of the whole discussion, trying to avoid definite association with either of the two potentially hostile *blocs*. As has already been pointed out, apropos of the Sino-Indian incidents, it takes more than a decision to be neutral to make neutrality a fact. It also requires the potential aggressor to refrain from aggression. The small movement in favour of world government is hardly more realistic. For all the obstacles already discussed that at present stand in the way of a world peace policy, and a good many more as well, would also stand in the way of world government. If the countries of the world were thinking along those lines the problem would already be on the way to being settled. Nor is the argument that world government is a more permanently satisfactory objective than mere attempts to prevent war any more convincing. Like the objective of peace, it is still too far away to give us any guidance as to policies in the months and years immediately ahead. How are we to decide what policies will bring us nearer to the objective, and how are we to make them possible, even if we can define them?

The fourth answer is that given by, or implicit in, the western European organizations that have grown up since 1948, in particular, those to which the nine members of the European Economic Community belong. This answer is essentially that, until such time as we can find some way of solving the problem of East–West relations, or as part of the preparation for that time, we should at least set our own house in order. In western Europe, a great many of the obstacles to closer union either do not exist, or are less intractable than they are elsewhere. These are countries that have a shared history and similar traditions and have reached similar stages of economic, social and political evolution. In 1976, all are democracies and mixed economies with capitalist free enterprise and State-controlled planning, in societies with a high standard of living. Their approach to international problems is similar. They could, therefore, set off on the road to what might, at least in theory, become one day a single *bloc*, economically and perhaps partially politically unified.

The idea has obvious attractions. It is positive. It can also help to raise the European standard of living and so enable the richer nations of the world to do more to help the poorer. During its short period of existence, the movement for European integration has indeed made considerable progress in the economic field. Whether this has really brought political integration any nearer is less certain, for reasons that have already been discussed. All that can be said, so far, is that the movement has established a claim to be here to stay. Where it is going may well be dependent on circumstances, as well as on men.

For one thing, "Europeanism" has not yet eliminated economic conflicts of interest between European nations, and it has created new political conflicts. It has added one more to the differences of opinion between the Western and Eastern *blocs*; it has divided the Europe on this side of the Iron Curtain

into partners whose economic and political problems differ
sufficiently to transform the everyday working of Community
institutions into an endless battle between conflicting national
interests and conflicting views regarding both the ultimate
goal of Europe and the pace and scope of the steps that
should be taken in the relatively near future to bring that
goal nearer. There is no unanimity, for instance, regarding
what ought to be the place of the European partners in the
NATO alliance. There has been conflict regarding the desirability of enhancing the status of the European Assembly
(miscalled the European Parliament) by providing for the
direct election of its members by European constituencies,
instead of continuing the present system of nomination of
the members by the national Parliaments. Even if this question
is settled in principle, there is no guarantee that agreement
will be reached about the much more important question of
the future powers of the Assembly.

Even within each country there are divisions of opinion
about these problems. Communists, for instance (and they
represent strong forces in France and Italy), were for long
opposed to the European movement on principle, seeing it as
essentially anti-Soviet. And this it certainly was, in so far as
Communists were unrepresented in the Community's organizations up to 1969. Many non-Communists, too, were anxious
lest the development of integration in the Community should
harden the division between the Europes on each side of the
Iron Curtain, and, in particular, make even less likely the
future reunification of Germany. In Great Britain, the division
between those who were for and those who were against British
membership was caused partly by differing estimates of the
economic advantages of membership, but partly also by fears
that membership might prove incompatible with membership
of the Commonwealth. British opponents of membership were
afraid of losing a multi-racial, world-wide association, with

---

[1] Hawtrey. *Western European Union* (Royal Institute of International Affairs), p. 40.

all its potentialities for bringing haves and have-nots, East and West, closer, and of finding that the European Economic Community was not only a closed economic society, a club to make the rich richer, but also a closed political society, which would inevitably be regarded by the under-developed nations as a club of privileged great powers.

Controversy in Britain regarding the pros and cons of membership and the terms on which it should be sought continued with varying intensity from well before 1961, when the Government made the first application to join the E.E.C., to June 1975 when, two and a half years after British membership had finally become effective, a referendum was held to decide whether or not the nation wished to remain in the Community. How was the ordinary citizen, without understanding of the complex economic problems involved, to make up his mind on what ought to be done? Similar arguments, and others as well were going on between the other members of the Community, who had, in addition to the difficulties of absorbing the new members, economic and political problems of their own to contend with, on which they were profoundly divided.

It would be a mistake, however, to conclude that difficulties and misunderstandings on this scale necessarily mean either that the European movement is in danger of imminent collapse, or that the average citizen is in danger of wanting to wash his hands of it, and leave everything in the hands of the Community bureaucracy. All these opinions and attitudes represent only the early stages of attempts to get away from the anarchic nationalism of the nineteenth century and the first half of the twentieth, to find methods by which men can, if only gradually, move towards a more rational international society. It would be as unrealistic to dismiss them as it would be to entertain optimistic illusions regarding the possibility of rapid progress. Nationalism is centuries old and attempts to create really effective international organizations are only in their infancy. The citizen of the late twentieth century is living in a period of more rapid and profound economic and political change than our civilization has yet known, not only owing to nuclear discoveries, electronics, automation, and the exploration of space, but also owing to the creation during the past ten years of large numbers of independent states, most of which have to face incredibly difficult economic as well as political problems. The future is, therefore, more than ever before, full of unknowns, and consequently of hopes, fears, speculations, theories and experiments. The new nations are trying to find their feet; the old nations are trying to keep their heads and adapt themselves to the new circumstances.

In the meantime, whether or not the average citizen is able to contribute effectively to the international argument, he still has his responsibilities in relation to the future of his own State. In the following chapters, therefore, we shall return to some of the basic problems that face the individual in his efforts to be a good citizen.

PART TWO

Man and his Fellow Citizens

CHAPTER SIX

Man as a Social Animal

ARISTOTLE's conclusion that man is a political animal has not only become a commonplace of political theory, it is an assumption which is essential to the theory and practice of democracy. If man were not a political animal, then it would be useless to expect him to understand political issues and to develop the sense of civic responsibility on which democracy must rely if it is to be effective. It is possible, however, for democratic systems to expect too much from the citizen, to regard him, in effect, exclusively as a political animal. Some social reformers, and Socialist reformers in particular, have concentrated so much of their attention on the need to provide truly democratic institutions, in which the citizen could play his full part, that they have tended to forget that the average man or woman thinks about politics for a very small percentage of the time. If we were to take a Gallup poll of men's interests, it is highly probable that, in Great Britain at least, politics would come a long way down the list. This may be an unpalatable conclusion, but it is one that social reformers will have to take into account, if institutions are to be adapted to the needs of citizens, instead of being devised to satisfy the requirements of political theorists.

It seems unlikely that, even with more widely diffused educational opportunities, more than a small minority of citizens will take an active interest in politics. Politics are, as we have seen, a framework, a means to certain ends such as the creation of social justice, or, to use Bentham's phrase, to "the maximization of pleasure and the minimization of pain". It is only natural that men should be more conscious of their own desires than of the means by which those desires can be satisfied. They are born into a State which already has its rules and traditions, into a nation whose way of life they are bound to take more or less for granted, in the same way as they take for granted the background of family and school in which they grow up. By the time they are old enough to reflect about these things, they have already been deeply influenced by them in a thousand different ways and can look at them objectively only as the result of a conscious effort, which relatively few have either the time or the intellectual equipment to make with any degree of thoroughness. To most people, politics are remote from their ordinary lives. It is only when they are brought up against political realities, by the realization that they are being prevented from doing something that they want to do, or forced to do things that they do not want to do, that they become conscious that it is political action which creates the conditions which govern their lives. In the long run, Governments depend on the will of the citizens, but, except in periods of crisis, the citizen is far more conscious of being the done-to than the doer.

Up to now, we have been discussing the relations between the citizen and the State, primarily from the point of view of the student of politics who is anxious to discover some general rules governing the organization of political societies. It is equally important to look at the problems of political societies from the point of view of the individual citizen, considered not merely as a political animal, but as a social animal, with complex social relationships in which politics and the State often appear to play only a small part. The fact that he may take for granted most of the rules which, as we have seen, control his activities from birth to death and from dawn to dusk means that he may remain for most of his life unaware of the extent to which he needs the co-operation of the State in order to fulfil his personal ambitions. Even if he is aware of his political responsibilities, he is not a political animal all the time. He will be, in the main, far more aware of the non-political aspects of what interests him than he will of the complex network of legislation which enables him and thousands of his fellow citizens to pursue their professions and hobbies without coming into conflict with each other or with the State.

The political machinery of democracy already takes some account of these non-political activities of the citizen. During any British election campaign, candidates are inundated with appeals from different organizations, asking for assurances that their demands will be supported by the candidate, should he be elected. And if he is, they will continue to bombard him with appeals for support in the House of Commons, if any question concerning their activities is to be raised. Candidates do not appeal for the votes of citizens, as individuals, merely by outlining the policy of their party on the principal national or international issues. They often appeal as well to sections of the community whose dominant interests are non-political, to religious sects, for example, or motorists, or housewives. They calculate their chances of obtaining the votes of tradesmen, old age pensioners, the middle classes, civil servants, Catholics, Nonconformists, Jews and so on, all of whom have some special interest, not necessarily related directly to the policies of any political party. Sectional interests often bring pressure to bear on both Members of Parliament and political parties in order to obtain for themselves conditions that will enable them to pursue more freely purposes that have little or nothing to do with politics.

Pressure of this kind is held to be legitimate, surely, because the State recognizes that individuals have a part to play outside their direct contribution to the processes of government. The State has not merely the negative duty of arbitrating between competing claims, but also the positive duty of finding ways in which individuals and groups can best fulfil themselves, in so far, of course, as their purposes do not conflict with the purposes of the State.

In the modern State, this is no easy task, because the growth of communications, of industry and trade have so speeded up and complicated political processes that not only the ordinary citizen, but also the ordinary back-bench Member of Parliament, feels that he has no longer either the knowledge or the time to understand and control sufficiently the application of the major items of policy, let alone to consider a number of extraneous issues, often having little bearing on general policy. Nor is it possible for Parliament to devote to these sectional and individual interests the time that it could afford to give to them when legislation was a placid and unhurried affair, preceded by lengthy debates in which there was ample opportunity for the expression of individual views—debates, moreover, which could still influence the vote. For party divisions were less rigid, speakers had the time to develop their arguments, and the House had the time to listen.

The modern citizen, whether his interests are primarily political or not, often feels that he has less and less opportunity to make his voice heard and to make his personal contribution to the affairs of the community. The fact that Parliament is overworked and has virtually no time to devote to subjects not directly related to party policy makes it difficult for him to find a place for his personal interests in the general pattern of politics. This is not to say that discussion of these subjects in Parliament constitutes either an adequate, or even a suitable method of recognizing their importance. But it might help to stimulate political interest in those who at present are not interested in political processes, and so lead to more imaginative ways of recognizing the value of the contribution that all individuals and groups can make to the well-being of the community as a whole. The citizen who is actively interested in politics is often in no more enviable a position. At a time when Members of Parliament have to consider in a single session some eighty or more complicated Public Bills, most of them very technical (requiring months to be transformed into Acts of Parliament), it is impossible either for them or for their constituents to devote even to major items of policy the degree of attention that would be required in order to make a truly personal contribution.

The process of modern government seems to the average citizen to have become more and more a matter for technicians, bureaucrats and experts of all kinds, something which it is difficult for him to understand and still more difficult to argue about. It is easier to grasp consequences than causes, to see muddle, slowness, inhumanity or injustice than to understand how the cumbrous machinery of government works and what is or is not humanly possible at any particular time and at what cost. The citizen may well end by becoming impatient with the whole process, because he feels himself to be a powerless victim, instead of an essential part of the machine. As the scope of State action extends, the scope of local or regional organs of government is either restricted or complicated by a mass of new regulations governing their relations with the State. As Governments become more overworked, citizens become less interested. There is what the nineteenth-century Frenchman, Lamennais, described as "apoplexy at the centre and anæmia at the extremities".

We are not concerned here with institutional proposals to remedy the apoplexy at the centre—proposals for devolution, decentralization, the reform of procedure and the like. It is the anæmia at the extremities, the apathy of the ordinary citizen, which concerns us. How can he be made to feel that he has an individual contribution to make to the democratic process and how can we find effective channels through which he can make it?

One solution is to use new techniques of consultation. We are not considering now the citizen who is an active politician and so we need not consider purely political devices, such as the recall of Members of Parliament, or the referendum, or proposals for reform of the electoral system. The non-political or a-political citizen usually needs to make his impact felt on only a few specific points. Parents, housewives, property owners, small shopkeepers, motorists, cyclists, members of rambling clubs, gardening enthusiasts, may have something to contribute to the process of democratic government at the point at which it touches their special interests. They have special needs, problems, perhaps grievances; and they need to be satisfied that they can, if need be, make their voices effectively heard. As we saw in Chapter Two, there is hardly any sector of social life that is not affected more or less directly by the action of the State, or by the local government authority, which is the equivalent of the State in matters of local concern. We all have an interest in some facets of community life. The difficulty is to find appropriate channels for the expression of these interests and to devise suitable machinery for the utilization of individual capacities which are at the moment not sufficiently associated with civic or political fields of activity.

Admittedly the task will not be easy. For it is essential that the State shall not make excessive demands on the citizen and at the same time that whatever democratic machinery is devised shall not be used merely to pretend to consult individuals, while in reality ignoring what they have to say. Too often, consultative organs come to be regarded by the public as being little more than a façade behind which powerful interests can always get their way. One method of helping the citizen to recover his citizenship, or to make fuller use of it, is, of course, to find ways of enabling him to participate more actively in the processes of local government. It has often been suggested that, now that essential functions such as transport, gas, electricity, health and education are becoming to an increasing extent the responsibility either of the larger local authorities or of central Government departments, the citizen's interest in local government has inevitably declined. Many local committees have become little more than administrative instruments of a policy that is to all intents and purposes decided on the national level. If the citizen's interest in local government is to be revived, new fields of activity will have to be found. It has been suggested, for example, that local authorities could do more to encourage local theatres, improve their sports facilities, provide for holiday amusements in parks, and, in general, concentrate more of their attention on increasing local amenities, now that the essential services no longer require so much of their attention.

This could be a valuable outlet for individual and social initiative, if and when resources become available. It is possible, too, for citizens who are not directly interested in the problems of local administration to share in the work of voluntary associations, such as Youth Clubs, Citizens' Advice Bureaux, Civil Defence organizations, the N.S.P.C.C., the R.S.P.C.A., the National Council of Social Service, the National Council of Women, the W.V.S., all of which have, or could have, local committees which could use the initiative and capacities of interested citizens.

Those who have no special interests or capacities that can usefully or suitably be associated with the work of organs of government or of local or national voluntary social organizations, or who do not want to share in this kind of work, are sometimes glad to join social community associations. These already exist in many places and more could be set up if there were a demand for them. "Being democratic," says G. D. H. Cole, "is not the same thing as holding advanced opinions. It is not the same thing as believing in democracy. It starts with knowing your neighbours as real persons. . . . The real democracy that does exist in Great Britain . . . is to be found for the most part, not in Parliament or in the institutions of local government, but in the smaller groups, formal or informal, in which men and women join together out of decent fellowship or for the pursuit of a common social purpose—societies, clubs, churches, and not least, informal neighbourhood groups."

The idea of neighbourliness as a means whereby the modern citizen can escape from the feeling that he is a little man in a big world has already been developed in several ways. Modern town planning tries to take into account the need to create this sense of belonging to a community, by breaking down new towns into neighbourhood units, each with its shopping centre, school and church, and local hall for social functions. Local authorities in many places are doing what they can to see that the physical conditions for creating community centres exist, such as suitable buildings. One has only to think of the difference that Women's Institutes have made to life in many villages, or of what Youth Clubs have done and are still doing for adolescents in some towns, to realize how much could be done, given the physical facilities and the right imaginative approach to the problem.

The problem concerns large towns, of course, more than villages, but it is precisely in towns that such action is most difficult to stimulate. It would be foolish to suggest that the enormous problems created and perpetuated by bad homes, bad housing, racial friction, juvenile delinquency, and so on, can be dealt with by amenities, good will and either professional or amateur "do-gooding". It would also be unrealistic to expect overburdened Governments and local authorities to exercise much initiative in these fields, while they remain unable to meet some of the most pressing social needs—for homes, hospitals, schools, for instance. And all the more so in periods of economic crisis, inflation or mass unemployment. Nor, even in favourable conditions, is the problem of political apathy, on the local as well as the national level, likely to be easily solved.

The locality is not, however, the only possible focus of interest. In towns and suburbs it is difficult for citizens to develop a real sense of community, and this is perhaps why some politicians and social reformers tend more and more to seek a remedy for political and social apathy in what has come to be called "participation", that is, the creation of institutions concentrating more on the focus of the individual's professional interests. Men could be given a more creative interest in their work through the

medium of appropriate functional organizations which provided them with opportunities to make their specialist contribution to the community. It may be argued that such organizations already exist and are either not used or are misused.
There is the Trade Union, whose branch meetings are so often
attended only by a faithful few, or by members who want to
use the organization for political rather than industrial and
professional purposes. Many Trade Unionists are apathetic
for the same reason that many members of political parties
are apathetic. They feel themselves to be unimportant units
in a great machine. But in the workshop, the store, the school
or the office, they could often be members of associations to
which they could make a real individual contribution. There
are local Chambers of Commerce, Parent-Teacher Associations, for example, which do much to make their members
conscious, not only of the comradeship of the group, but also
of the impact that one individual can make on a group, when
it is united by common interests.

Even where permanent organizations are not wanted, or
not feasible, it is often possible to consult interested or expert
citizens on specific questions as they crop up. Harold Laski
proposed the setting up of a whole network of advisory committees which could be consulted by either Parliamentary or
local departments. Such committees would consist of panels
of individuals, prepared to give their advice on subjects on
which they had either specialized knowledge or in which they
were particularly interested. Governments would then be
able to take these views into account before legislation was
drafted, instead of leaving it to the hazards of debate to discover what ordinary people thought of their proposals, as
distinct from the opinions of powerful interests, directly
affected and able to make their views known. Something
has been done to give effect to these proposals in the thirty
years or so since Laski first put them forward. For instance, the
Gas, Electricity and Coal Boards have their committees to
keep the authorities in touch with the opinions of the ordinary

consumer. But we have some distance to travel before we can be said to have fulfilled the purpose he set. "We need," he wrote in 1925, "to universalize that experiment for every department of administration where it is likely to prove creative. For the more we can convince the body of citizens of their direct interest in the process of politics, the better is likely to be the result of political effort."

It is possible to object to these, and indeed to all the above suggestions, on the ground that they assume, as social reformers tend too easily to assume, that the average man (or woman) is prepared to spend his few leisure hours sitting on innumerable committees. If he were, then a great many of the problems of citizenship would resolve themselves. For many of the activities mentioned above are already open to the citizen who is interested enough to take the trouble to find out how to join them. And many more need only the initiative of a few enthusiasts to be transformed from apathetic or ineffective groups to vital and live associations. The citizen who wants, that is *consciously* wants, to find opportunities to practise his citizenship will not have any serious difficulty in doing so. The difficulty lies in stimulating the desire. Yet if we are not successful in stimulating it, democracy must end by being an experiment that failed. After all, in the last resort, the quality of our democracy is determined by the quality of the average citizen. We get the Government we deserve in the sense that no Government can go faster than its electors will allow.

It is possible, however, for institutions to help the citizen to become conscious of his responsibilities, to provide an initial stimulus which to-day seems only too often lacking. It is easy enough to blame either State or citizen; to argue that the modern State does so much for the citizen that he has lost all desire to do anything for himself; or to argue that responsible citizenship of the kind that we have been discussing is a Utopian ideal that has never been realized and is never likely to be realized. It may be true that the State is not helping the citizen, or rather some citizens, in the right way. Before we are tempted to conclude that democracy has failed, it is as well to remind ourselves, as has already been said, that it is still a comparatively new experiment. It is at least a tenable hypothesis that we have not yet found the right techniques to interest important sections of the community. It would be understandable if this were so. Great changes in our social and economic environment have followed so rapidly on the heels of the democratization of the political system, that we may need a generation or two in which to catch up and to adapt our thinking to the changed conditions. It has been suggested that we need far more than the kind of opportunity for individual participation that has been discussed in this chapter; local government, for example, may need much more than superficial adaptations. It may be necessary to think out afresh what ought to be its functions in the modern world and to recast many of its institutions. Local government areas often seem to bear little relation to living communities; the responsibilities of local councillors seem at times far too onerous, at others too trivial; we may need a wholly new approach to the problem of the government of large agglomerations and also to the very different problems of rural areas.

One of the responsibilities of the student of politics is precisely to do his share of this necessary thinking, to work out where there are gaps and inadequacies in our democratic institutions. For if democracy assumes that we are all of equal worth as individuals, it does not assume that we have all an equal contribution to make towards the discovery of the best techniques of democratic government. That must be the responsibility of those who are already politically minded. To quote G. D. H. Cole again, "a society, whatever its formal structure, cannot be democratic unless a goodly number of men and women do take an interest in keeping it so."

Nor should such thinking be concentrated exclusively on

institutional problems. The grant of rights and the existence of appropriate institutions to enforce them constitute only half the battle. Victory comes only when we are educated to use our rights properly. It is no less true to-day than it was in 1867 that we must educate our masters. One of the ways in which we may help the citizen both to be more conscious of the potential worth of his individual contribution to the success of the democratic experiment and to be readier to seek new ways of playing his part as a citizen is by providing more adequate and attractive educational opportunities, and particularly more opportunities to understand how intimately politics affect him personally. The teaching of civics in schools; the provision of Forces' educational broadcasts on political and social questions; these, along with better facilities for adult education, constitute a beginning, but little more than that. If we are to attract more than a potentially politically-minded fringe of the population we shall need to provide more imaginatively thought out inducements to forsake the cinema and television programmes.

Neither institutional reforms nor educational facilities, however well thought out they may be, can make democracy a success until the citizen becomes actively aware of the ways in which public affairs impinge upon his private affairs and decides to do what he can about it in the particular spheres of activity that are open to him. When he begins to ask himself whether the State is providing him with adequate scope for self expression; when he asks whether he has as good a chance as the next man of enjoying family life, of obtaining adequate intellectual and moral equipment for life, of making use of his abilities, and if not why not, then he is well on the way to becoming an intelligent citizen who will make use of institutions and of educational opportunities to get what he wants or to try to change the system so that it will give him what he wants. There will always be limits to what can be done by State action but, in a democracy, the citizen can at least ensure that all politics can do to give him a square deal, to see that he is not more of a square peg in a round hole than his neigh-bour, is actually being done. In the following chapters we shall try to discuss what people have thought politics can or ought to do to help the citizen to develop fully the poten-tialities of his personality, and some of the implications of their views for present-day citizens.

CHAPTER SEVEN

The Fundamental Rights of the Citizen

THE history of political thought points to a persistent belief in men that States ought to guarantee to individuals the enjoyment of a certain number of basic human rights, which constitute the essential conditions of "the good life". In any discussion of rights, there are two distinctions that we must bear constantly in mind. We must distinguish, first, between moral and legal rights, between what we think *ought* to be our rights and what, in fact, *are* our rights. Moral rights do not necessarily bear much relation to the rights which have been legally or constitutionally recognized by actual States, during the course of history. "A true moral right," says Hobhouse, "is one which is demonstrably justifiable by relation to the common good, whether it is actually recognized or not." Unfortunately, the word 'demonstrably' begs the question. Demonstrably to whom? If the claim does not appear to those in power in the State to be "demonstrably justifiable", then obviously it will not be recognized, and it may not be recognized even if it does, for States often fail to live up to their ideals. Legal and constitutional rights represent a minimum which people have either agreed to accept or been compelled to put up with, moral rights a maximum which they believe would be attained, if the country were properly run. The second distinction we must make is between theoretical and enforceable rights. It is important to note the form in which rights are granted. The statement, in a constitution or elsewhere, that certain specified rights are guaranteed will remain totally without effect, if there is no way by which the citizen can see that the State does, in actual fact, guarantee his enjoyment of them. States sometimes use such paper guarantees as a device by which to evade obligations which public opinion wants to compel them to assume. Rights are accorded on paper, but the necessary steps to implement them are never taken, or texts are framed in such a way as to defeat the expressed intention.

For centuries, there has been in almost all civilized States a persistent and widespread conviction that some rights are so essential to the fulfilment of the individual's personality that they can be called "natural rights". They are held to be "natural", in the sense that their recognition is implicit in the facts of social organization or in the sense that they are beyond argument. In point of fact, however, there has been a great deal of argument about them. Men have disagreed about rights, as they have disagreed about everything under the sun. For example, a British writer has claimed that "six months' scrutiny of a correspondence column revealed a natural right to a living wage, a right to work, a right to trial by jury, a right to buy cigarettes after eight p.m., a right to camp in a caravan by the roadside, and a right to walk on the grouse moors of Scotland during the close season."[1]

Generally speaking, however, men have been agreed on the need for recognition of a number of fundamental rights, although they have not always been agreed as to what they were. In the eighteenth century, it was expected that agreement would ultimately be reached on this point, because it was assumed that human nature was the same everywhere. The French revolutionaries of 1789 described the rights which they were claiming for French citizens as a "Declaration of the rights of man and the citizen". The Declaration of Independence, by the representatives of the United States assembled in Congress on July 4th, 1776, was primarily a

---

[1] Quoted by Mabbott, *The State and the Citizen* (Hutchinson's University Library), p. 58n.

statement of the reasons which had led these States to sever their allegiance to the British crown. But it affirmed that, in the opinion of the signatories, certain truths were "self-evident". "We hold these truths to be self-evident", they said "that all men are created equal; that they are endowed by their Creator with inalienable rights; that among these rights are life, liberty, and the pursuit of happiness."

If we look more closely at these two documents we see that, although there are only thirteen years between them, the rights which are assumed to be universal, to be "inalienable", are not the same for Frenchmen and for Americans. We can really reduce to five the rights that are claimed in these two documents. They are the rights to equality, liberty, property, happiness and the right not to be taxed without consent. But not all of them are claimed by each, and the emphasis, the spirit in which they are claimed, differs considerably. Both assert that men are born free and equal and with certain rights, which it is the duty of Governments to safeguard. But, while the American Declaration speaks of "life, liberty, and the pursuit of happiness", the French Declaration makes no mention of happiness and is primarily concerned with the need to protect liberty and property, to prevent individuals from being arbitrarily arrested or punished, and to ensure that taxation is not imposed without the consent of the citizens. There is a great deal of common ground between the French Declaration and the American Constitution, if we include the amendments which were added to the latter in 1791. Both recognize the right to freedom of opinion and religion (American first Amendment; French Declaration, Article X); to security of the person against arbitrary arrest and to security of personal property (French Declaration, Articles VII and XVII; American Amendment IV); both consider that the people's will is the source of all law and that no individual should be penalized, except in pursuance of laws approved by the whole community (French Declaration, Article III; American Amendments V and IX). But while the French were anxious to protect the citizen from the particular kinds of arbitrary interference with his liberty which were characteristic of eighteenth-century France—the *lettres de cachet*, the excessive taxation, the persecution of political and religious opinions—the Americans were preoccupied with a different set of problems, with the billeting of soldiery on citizens without their permission and without legal authority, with the right of the several States not to be submerged in the Union to such an extent that they lost their separate identity, with the rights of individuals to form associations to express their opinions. In both cases, immediate grievances, which were essentially transitory, were felt so strongly that remedies for them were included in documents claiming to represent universal and permanent rights.

In seventeenth-century England, Locke, too, had assumed that certain rights were "natural". Indeed, he believed that the rights which the Social Contract was designed to protect were both natural to man and approved by God. "The law of Nature," he says, "stands as an eternal rule to all men, legislators as well as others. The rules that they make for other men's actions must, as well as their own and other men's actions, be conformable to the law of Nature—i.e., to the will of God, of which that is a declaration, and the fundamental law of Nature being the preservation of mankind, no human sanction can be good or valid against it." In Locke's view, the legitimate purpose of all power was the preservation of mankind, which meant that men's fundamental rights included the right not to be destroyed, enslaved or designedly impoverished by the State. He also held that "the supreme power cannot take from any man any part of his property without his own consent. For the preservation of property being the end of government, and that for which men enter into society, it necessarily supposes and requires that the people should have property. . . ."[1]

---

[1] Second Treatise, § 138.

It is not possible here to consider the impact of theology on men's conceptions of their rights. Whatever may have been adduced as the reasons for claiming this or that right as a moral or "natural" right, what interests us here is primarily the nature of the claim and the extent to which it has been met by actual States. We have a relatively clear idea of what the majority of civilized nations, to-day, consider ought to be the fundamental rights of mankind, for there have been two recent formulations of minimum human demands. They are, first, the Atlantic Charter of 1941, which included among the allied war aims the achievement of four freedoms: freedom of speech and belief and freedom from fear and want; and second, the Universal Declaration of Human Rights, passed and proclaimed by the General Assembly of the United Nations on December 10th, 1948. This latter document lays down a minimum standard of human rights, based on "the inherent dignity" and the "equal and inalienable rights of all members of the human family". It affirms that all human beings ought to be treated as equals, and as having a fundamental right to individual liberty. In accepting these principles, nations ought, therefore, to refuse to make distinctions between individuals on the ground of their birth, race, religion, wealth or status. Individuals ought everywhere to be treated as equal in dignity and rights, and these rights ought to include political rights, including the right to participate in the government of their country, and professional rights, including access on equal terms to the public services. Nations ought to safeguard liberty by protecting individuals from slavery, torture, arbitrary arrest, and from discrimination of any kind not made on account of infringements of clearly defined laws, proved to the satisfaction of independent tribunals. The right to personal liberty ought to entitle people to move about freely inside their country and to leave it and return as they wish.

The declaration also includes the right to nationality, the right to choose a wife (or a husband), to found a family and to have some say in the way the children are to be brought up, the right to practise the religion of one's choice and to express one's views freely, either on religion or any other subject, the right to join with other people to form associations. Among economic rights, the declaration mentions the right to own property, to work for one's living, and the right of specially needy categories of the population—the sick, the unemployed, widows, and children—to receive aid from the State. It claims the right of all to receive equal pay for equal work, equal rights to education, and the right of everybody to protect his interests through a Trade Union.

Now if we look at the practice of a number of the States which approved this declaration, it will be clear at once that they are interpreting very differently their common undertaking to "strive by teaching and education to promote respect for these rights and freedoms and, by progressive measures, national and international, to secure their universal and effective recognition and observance". Russia refused to sign it, which is a comprehensible attitude, since she does not believe in the principles of individual liberty as the majority of the members of the United Nations understand them. Mr. Vyshinsky said that Russia would never sign a declaration recognizing freedom of speech and movement. Russian trials, Russian prison camps constitute visible and tangible evidence of a denial of both the spirit and the letter of the declaration. There are differences of practice, however, among the signatories too. Americans would no doubt consider that the class distinctions which exist in Great Britain infringed the principle of equality, whereas both British and Americans have been charged with infringements of the principle of equality between races. In almost every country there are customs or procedures which other countries would hold to be infringements of one or another of the articles of the Universal Declaration.

If we compare its terms with those of earlier declarations that have been mentioned, it is clear, too, that there are a

number of rights which, to-day, are held to be natural or
normal, but which had not even been thought of a century
and a half ago. In the eighteenth century, rights were thought
of in almost exclusively political terms. The battle for economic
equality had hardly begun. The Preambles of the French
Constitutions of 1946 and 1958 are much nearer to the spirit of
the Universal Declaration than to that of the Declaration of
the Rights of Man of 1789, not because the French would
repudiate that document to-day, but because they now believe
that political rights alone cannot achieve the equality and
liberty which were claimed as fundamental rights in 1789.
The Preambles to these two modern Constitutions therefore
reformulate fundamental rights in terms of what are now
believed to be their social and economic, as well as their
political implications.

What all this suggests is that the concept of "natural rights"
is, has always been and must remain subjective. Rights are
"self-evident" only in their own time and place and, even
then, only if expressed in vague and general terms that, in
practice, mean different things to different people. If we think
of claims to fundamental rights as a kind of song sung by the
human race through history, then as long as we look only at
the words, it seems to be much the same song. But nations
have sung it to widely differing tunes. Wherever people
have demanded the right to liberty, equality, association,
security, freedom from want, or freedom from fear, the
claimants have had at the back of their minds a more or less
precise picture of the ways in which they thought the principles ought to be applied. Or, to change the metaphor, if we
think of rights as a kind of abstract lay figure, then, in the
imagination of the claimants, it is clothed, sometimes in the
contemporary fashion, sometimes in clothes of their own
designing. For example, France has always attached importance to a clear statement of the principles which, in the
opinion of Frenchmen, States ought to strive to apply. The
British have felt it less necessary to define their rights in general

terms than to ensure that a British citizen who felt he was being deprived of his rights had the practical means of claiming their enforcement. But in applying these respective principles, both nations have had blind spots which, in practice, have helped to render much of what they tried to achieve ineffective. The French have tended to concentrate so much of their attention on the theoretical definition of their rights that they have not always been sufficiently conscious of the gap between their theory and their practice. The British, with all their insistence on the need for practical means of enforcement, have not always been sufficiently conscious of the fact that only a small number of British citizens were able to use the machinery. Most British politicians in the early nineteenth century thought that the disfranchised, the illiterate, the farm labourer, the town artisan or factory worker were less able than their social superiors to determine what their rights were, and they took it as normal and proper that the wealthier classes should speak for the others. Locke thought that the State ought to protect the individual's property, and British law does, in fact, contain numerous, complex, and detailed provisions designed to achieve this end. But Locke would not have understood the claim of a propertyless farm labourer to the right to possess some of the property which the State was protecting so efficiently for his landlord. It is only fair to add that, with very few exceptions, such as the seventeenth century Levellers and agrarian Communists, the farm labourers thought it no less normal and right that the land should belong to the landlord. Later on, however, they changed their minds on this and many other things that the seventeenth and eighteenth centuries took for granted. By the middle of the nineteenth century a number of people in Europe had decided that the farm labourer's right to the land was, even more than his landlord's, natural, self-evident, in accordance with the will of God or the principles of immutable justice. There were landlords who justified their right to keep what they had on the same principles, or who argued that their possession was justified because they had owned the land for generations, or because their country's greatness was due to leadership by generations of landowners, or because all great civilizations had had a privileged *élite*. All of these would probably have subscribed willingly and sincerely to a general charter of rights, paying tribute to the principles of liberty, equality or fraternity (at any rate to the first two; fraternity has always come a bad third, even in theory). The difficulty would be to discover exactly what they meant by the terms, and precisely how they thought the principles could be applied.

Nations have often replied to the demand for the recognition of rights by inscribing them in a constitution. In theory, the citizen ought then to know where he stands, though in practice, he is often far from sure. In formulating constitutional rights, constitution-makers have their mental reservations, in the same way as those who claim natural rights, and so the measures introduced by Governments in order to enforce the constitutional provisions do not always succeed in applying the principles and sometimes do not even try.

The British citizen is under a different kind of disability. He can usually, though not always, discover what his legal rights are in particular cases, but these will not enable him to form a complete picture of his constitutional rights, and there is no document called a Constitution that he can consult. A British citizen can discover relatively simply what the law of the land will permit. If he tries to exercise his "right" to buy cigarettes out of hours, a court of law will punish him. If he is charged with an offence, the court will inform him whether or not he has the right to be tried by a jury. An employer who pays him less than the statutory wage, where one exists, can be compelled to comply with the law. But a British citizen may want an answer to the general question: What are my constitutional rights? In that case he is obliged to rely on the interpretations of constitutional lawyers and historians.

A French or an American citizen can back up his claim to rights by quoting the text of the Constitution. It is questionable, however, whether this will be of much assistance to him in trying to enforce them. The Frenchman will note that his fundamental rights are all enumerated, not in the body of the Constitution, but in the Preamble. He—or she—would have learned from the Preamble to the 1946 Constitution as also from that of 1958, that "the law guarantees to women rights equal in all respects to those of men." In fact, of course, French law did, and still does nothing of the kind. It gives fathers rights over their children which are denied to mothers. Unless married couples enter into a specific undertaking by which the wife retains control over her own money, it will be the husband who has the deciding voice in the control of the family finances. The husband's domicile, not the wife's, is considered to be the family domicile. Should she decide to accept employment in a town other than the one in which her husband lives, she may find that, as a married woman, she is obliged by law to obtain her husband's consent. If she tries to enforce her constitutional rights, she will discover that lawyers do not believe the provisions of Preambles to be legally enforceable. They are statements of principle, they say, reformulations of the principles of 1789, in more modern terminology. If a French Trade Unionist seeks to discover whether or not he has a constitutional right to strike, he will find this right recognized in the Preamble of the 1946 Constitution, "within the framework of the laws governing its exercise". No such laws were passed until 1963, and the law then voted covers only a limited number of cases.

An American citizen will not necessarily fare much better. True, the legal authority of the American Constitution is uncontested. But there are American rights, too, whose exercise is governed by "regulations", which have either not been drawn up, or which have been framed in such a way as to defeat the ostensible purpose of the constitutional provision granting the right. Thus, for example, Amendment XV states that: "the right of citizens of the United States to vote shall not be denied or abridged by the United States or by any State on account of race, colour, or previous condition of servitude." It goes on to say that "Congress shall have power to enforce this article by appropriate legislation". How did Congress enforce it? More than a third of the States of the Union imposed tax, educational or property qualifications, which, in practice, excluded thousands of negroes from exercising their constitutional right to vote. Massachussets imposed an educational test, Pennsylvania a tax qualification; a number of Southern States prohibited propertyless and illiterate citizens from voting, a provision expressly designed to exclude negroes. "For all practical purposes," wrote Charles and Mary Beard in 1930, "this section of the Constitution is a dead letter." It was only from 1954 onwards that a consistent attempt was made to prevent segregation of white and coloured children and students in American schools and universities in the South, and the battle is not yet won.

These are not the only examples that could be quoted of discrepancies between constitutional theory and practice. The Soviet Constitution of 1936 and the revised Constitution of 1947 both provided on paper for the exercise of a number of rights, of whose existence, to put it mildly, no observer can feel confident. If we look at the constitutions of the majority of modern democracies, it can be seen at once that certain rights are recognized in most of them, and that others are very generally recognized. Thus, freedom of speech and the press, freedom of conscience and religion, the right to individual liberty and fair legal processes, the right of assembly, the right to equality, education, property and social security, are all specifically guaranteed in almost every European country and in the United States and the Soviet Union as well.[1] Yet

---

[1] Denmark, Ireland, Italy, Portugal, the U.S.S.R., the Netherlands, Rumania, Czechoslovakia, Jugoslavia recognize all the rights enumerated above; Finland, Turkey, Belgium and Greece all but the right to social security; the U.S.A. all but the rights to social security and education; Bulgaria, all but the right of property. France recognizes all but the right of assembly, but in the Preamble, not in the text of the Constitution.

no one believes that these rights really exist in all these countries.

If, then, written constitutions can be by-passed and their intentions betrayed, if the British Constitution can be changed by the simple passage of an ordinary Act of Parliament (as happened, for example, in 1911 and 1949, when the powers of the House of Lords were radically curtailed), can it be argued that constitutional rights provide more effective guarantees than moral rights, inscribed in some declaration of principle which does not claim to possess any legal validity? In other words, are not both, equally, mere statements of intention?

To put the question in this way is to ignore the real function of a constitution. It is important to clear this point up.

Of themselves, constitutions cannot guarantee anything. Whether they work well or badly, whether they protect individual liberties zealously or inadequately, depends much less on the text of the constitution, on whether it is technically well or badly drawn up, than on the spirit in which it is applied by the men whose function it is to apply it. To repeat the metaphor employed earlier, we need to know the tune to which the politicians set the words before we can estimate correctly what the words mean. A constitution can only be a general framework, a statement of the guiding principles of government and of the machinery through which the principles are to be applied. It cannot be a set of tramlines along which Governments are forced, willy-nilly, to proceed. Constitutions allow more or less latitude for adaptation and improvisation. For ideas and needs change with the generations and if they are not adapted to respond to these changing needs, they become restrictive rather than liberating influences. On the other hand, if a constitution is too easy to change, it affords opportunities for unscrupulous Governments to abuse both its spirit and its letter.

Even with the best will in the world, the men who draw up, or who have to apply a constitution, cannot guarantee to make

it work well. There are circumstances in which *no* constitution
could work well. In the eighteenth century, Catherine of
Russia asked a French physiocrat, Mercier de la Rivière,
what was the best basis for the good government of a State.
He is said to have replied: "There is only one base, Madam:
the nature of things and of men." Things can defeat constitutional government as well as men. There are facts, both
physical and political, which a Government, however well
intentioned, may be powerless to change.

Constitutions are not perfect. They represent what the
constitution-makers were able to achieve in the circumstances,
and the circumstances are sometimes such that they do not
permit of a constitution which is at the same time acceptable
to the majority of opinion and easily workable. Constitutions
often leave out important things because the majority on
whom their acceptance depends cannot agree on them, or because attention was concentrated at the time on other things.
The French Constitutions of 1946 and 1958 made no mention
of the electoral system, because the parties could not agree
about it. The American Constitution provides for the election
of the President by the whole people, but indirectly, in two
stages. The people of the United States elect delegates whose
function is then to elect the President. At the time the constitution was drawn up, it was never assumed that the delegates would be party nominees, pledged to vote for the
candidate of the party which elected them. Yet that is how
it works to-day. The actual election of the President is a
formality, for, once the delegates have been elected, everyone knows that almost all are morally bound to vote in a
certain way. Then again, the makers of the American Constitution were anxious not to concentrate political power in
the hands of one body of men. They held that in order to avoid
the danger of tyranny, power ought to be divided between
several political organs. They, therefore, provided that the
Government should be responsible, not to Congress, but to
the President, and that the two elected Chambers should be

co-ordinate and be elected for different periods of office. These provisions do, of course, prevent any one of these organs from being the supreme repository of power. But since legislation requires the co-operation of President, Government and Legislature, they can also produce total deadlock, which is an eventuality that the constitution-makers never envisaged.

Nor are difficulties like this necessarily overcome, merely by making a constitution easy to change. There is still the problem of persuading people to agree to change it. Even in a democracy, men are not entirely masters of the constitution; they are also to some extent its prisoners. Whether they prefer a written or an unwritten, a rigid or a flexible constitution, the importance they attach to this or that provision— these are things that are not decided purely on the merits of the case, but in the light of the traditions, prejudices and symbolic values which have become associated in men's minds with both the form and the content of the constitution. They are traditions which have been very largely influenced by the fortunes or accidents of history. Thus, in Great Britain, which was for centuries secure from the danger of foreign invasion, people learnt to think of the Constitution as something which could be adapted slowly and peacefully to changing needs, without the need for any violent break with continuity. The possibility of evolution ruled out the need for revolution; and as evolution came to be more and more of a habit, revolution came to be more and more unthinkable. The parliamentary machine was at the same time toughened by accumulated traditions and made malleable by successive adaptations during centuries of almost uninterrupted parliamentary government. In eighteenth-century France, the revolutionaries who sought to replace absolutism by democracy were obliged to build the machinery through which the new principles were to be applied as they went along, and to subject it from the start, while it was still virtually untried, to the strain of a war in which the new system fought hostile neigh-

bours for its survival. From that time onwards, no system—
monarchic, imperial, or republican—was able to establish
itself firmly enough, or for long enough, to be able to develop
stable and tried institutions. As each régime was overthrown,
its successor tried to work out new constitutional machinery.
France acquired a unique collection of paper constitutions,
none of which lasted long enough to obtain the confidence of
all sections of the community. The British Constitution was
able to develop into an instrument accepted by all and capable
of being used equally effectively by opposing parties in the
State. French constitutions, on the other hand, remained in
people's minds inseparable from the parties, groups or factions
responsible for drawing them up, and so disappeared with
them. It has been said that all that was wrong with the Constitution of the Third Republic was that the men who governed
France did not use it properly. That may be an over-statement.
It is certainly true that one of the reasons which led the French
people to decide, in 1945, to make a new constitution, rather
than to reform the old, was that it was, for them, indissolubly
linked with the men who, they thought, had brought them
to disaster in 1940. In 1958, General de Gaulle decided to
change that Constitution, which he had always disliked.

Neither declarations of rights, then, nor constitutions can
effectively safeguard our rights, unless we have institutions
capable of enforcing the application of the principles that they
profess, and Governments and citizens determined to make
the institutions work properly. It was not until 1950 that the
first serious attempt was made to combine the need to express
belief in certain fundamental human freedoms, along the lines
of the Universal Declaration of Rights, with the need to create
international institutions capable of translating the intentions
into reality. On November 4th, 1950, the Committee of
Ministers of the Council of Europe signed in Rome a
"European Convention of Human Rights", described as
"Europe's Charter of Freedom". This document does more
than reaffirm some of the fundamental rights and freedoms

contained in the Universal Declaration; it goes on to define the precise organs and procedure by which the fifteen (later sixteen) signatories undertake to secure them to all within their jurisdiction. It is, in the words of the preamble, an attempt on the part of "the Governments of European countries which are likeminded and have a common heritage of political traditions, ideals, freedoms and the rule of law to take the first steps for the collective enforcement of certain of the Rights stated in the Universal Declaration."

These rights are: The right to life, liberty and the security of person (Universal Declaration Article 3, Convention Articles 2, 5); the right of persons who have been arrested or detained in accordance with a procedure prescribed by law to be presumed innocent until proved guilty, after a fair and public hearing, within a reasonable time, by an independent, impartial tribunal established by law, and after they have had full facilities to defend themselves (Universal Declaration 10, 11, Convention 5, 6); the right not to be held guilty of an offence which did not constitute a criminal offence under national or international law at the time it was committed (Universal Declaration 7, Convention 7); the right to respect for private and family life and correspondence (Universal Declaration 12, Convention 8); the rights to freedom of thought, conscience and religion, freedom of expression and peaceful assembly, including the right to join a Trade Union (Universal Declaration 9, 10, 11, 23, Convention 9, 10, 11); the right to marry and found a family (Universal Declaration 16, Convention 12); the right to obtain redress from a national authority in cases where these rights have been violated (Convention 13; the Universal Declaration 8, recognizes the right in cases of violation of "the fundamental rights granted by the constitution and the law"); and the right to enjoy them without discrimination on grounds of sex, race, religion, colour, political opinion or social status (Universal Declaration 2, Convention 14); the right not to be held in slavery or to be tortured or subjected to cruel, inhuman or degrading treatment or punishment (Universal Declaration 4, 5, Convention 3, 4).

The corresponding rights are, for the most part, worded in almost identical terms. There are, however, three important differences between the two documents. First, the Convention adds a number of detailed provisions, defining, for example, the circumstances in which exceptions to the rule may be permissible. Second, it is more cautious as well as more precise. In the Universal Declaration, for example, the right to marry and found a family is followed by the affirmation of the equal rights of men and women "during marriage and at its dissolution", and of the entitlement of the family to protection by society and the State. The Convention accords the right to marry and found a family only "according to the national laws governing the exercise of this right". This illustrates the ways in which the Convention seeks to be realistic. In some countries, to-day, sex equality, either in marriage or outside it, does not exist and, however morally desirable it may be that it should, it would be unrealistic to expect nations to enforce it here and now, merely because it is laid down in an international document. The Convention is cautious in statement because it seeks not to affirm rights that are in flat contradiction with national practice, but rather to ensure that rights which already exist in theory shall be enforced in practice. It is more precise in that it seeks to avoid formulation in terms so vague that they are virtually incapable of translation into agreed legal enactments. Thus, for example, the Convention omits the vague statement of the Universal Declaration concerning the right of the family "to protection by society and the State", for without further elaboration it is either meaningless or capable of an infinite number of meanings. Third, there are rights which nations to-day are not prepared to grant without question until the present international tension has lessened. Articles 15 and 16 of the Convention recognize this limiting factor and frankly admit that "in time of war or other public emergency threatening the life of the nation", signatory States may be compelled to take emergency security measures, in particular, to impose restrictions on the political activities of aliens which, in normal times, would be considered a violation of the obligation to make no racial or political distinctions.

Where the European Convention breaks new ground, however, is less in the first Section, devoted to the formulation of rights, than in Sections II to V, where it seeks to ensure that the rights shall be translated from paper into practice. It provides for their enforcement by two international bodies. The first is a European Commission of Human Rights, consisting of one representative from each member State, elected for six years by the Committee of Ministers, from a list submitted by the Consultative Assembly. The function of the Commission is to investigate complaints, where it considers them to be serious, either from member nations or from individuals or groups, regarding alleged violations of rights by member States.

The second is the European Court of Human Rights. It consists of one judge from each member State, elected for nine years by the Consultative Assembly from a list submitted by members of the Council of Europe. Its function is to hear cases brought before it either by member States or by the Commission, when the Commission believes that there has been a violation of human rights and has been unable to bring about a peaceful settlement.

How has this procedure worked in practice? Has it succeeded in establishing respect for these rights? Or does it seem on the way to succeeding?

It would be unrealistic to regard the European Convention as more than a timid and tentative attempt to tackle the problem of rights on the international level. The procedures, as outlined on paper, have not always worked in practice, because some member States have refused to bind themselves to accept the jurisdiction of the Court, or have limited their recognition of the right of the Commission to enquire into complaints regarding their failure to respect human rights. Thus, for instance, France, the country which under the Fifth Republic is more than all others laying claim to leadership in western Europe, refused to ratify her signature, and so, in effect, opted out altogether. Great Britain refused to recognize either the jurisdiction of the Court or the right of individual petition, as distinct from petition by Governments. Greece, Italy and Turkey adopted a similar attitude to that of Great Britain. Norway and Sweden refused to accept the jurisdiction of the Court.

It is easy enough to criticize these reservations, particularly on the part of Great Powers that might have been expected to give a lead. But it is precisely these Great Powers that have the most difficult problems to contend with. For years, France was sensitive to criticism, within either NATO or the United Nations, of her policies in Algeria. She was also sensitive to criticism from inside as well as from outside France, and, in particular, to allegations that the French army had been guilty of systematic use of torture in dealing with Algerian nationalist terrorists, and sometimes in dealing with members of the nationalist movement, whether or not they were suspected of terrorism. The Algerian problem was so difficult that the resources of French Governments were taxed to the uttermost, and no Government, of whatever political complexion, could have risked adding to its difficulties the complications of inter- ference from outside. Some critics were well-meaning, but ill- informed; but some deliberately distorted the truth for partisan ends. In a rebellion such as the Algerian war, where terrorism was one of the essential weapons of a small nationalist move- ment, there were bound to be wrongs and atrocities on both sides. No Government would, therefore, have risked submitting complaints to an international authority, in an effort to sort out truth from falsehood. British Governments were similarly sensitive to criticisms of their attitudes in Africa, or in Cyprus. Greece was sensitive to criticisms of her treatment of political prisoners. Does anyone seriously believe that any of the newly independent States would be any readier to submit problems felt to involve not only their national sovereignty, but perhaps also their national existence, to the arbitration of any so-called international tribunal? Would Kenya allow any international body to decide on the fairness or unfairness of her treatment of opposition politicians? Would Algeria submit the question of the rights of the French minority, deprived of their property by decrees alleged to be in flagrant violation of guarantees provided by the Evian Agreements, to be settled by any authority other than the Government of the sovereign Algerian Republic? The 1963 conflict between Algeria and Morocco was, it is true, settled by an international Commission. But both Algeria and Morocco were members of that Commission, and their consent to the settlement was therefore essential.

All this does not mean that the European Convention was useless. Its signatories have at least three positive achievements to their credit that can help to translate the "oughts" of human rights into "musts" in the international field. The first was their success in actually putting the Convention into operation. For years after the voting of the United Nations Universal Declaration, a Commission of Human Rights struggled without success to implement at least some of its provisions. Two draft Covenants, one dealing with political, the other with economic and social rights, were eventually drawn up. They provided, as did the European Convention, for limitations and exceptions to meet the opposition and reluctance of different States. But sixteen years after the passing of the Universal Declaration, neither had been brought into application. The European Convention came into force in 1953–4 and the Court heard its first case in 1960. In two cases submitted to the Court in the following two years, the Governments involved (those of Belgium and Ireland) both changed their policies so as to satisfy the requirements of the Convention. Some hundreds of complaints are submitted to the Commission every year.

The second achievement was to allow the Commission to receive complaints from individuals as well as from States. The United Nations Commission on Human Rights has been seriously restricted in its attempts to obtain information on infringements of human rights by the *de facto* obligation to seek

it only from Governments. Since some of the latter are considered in many quarters to be among the chief offenders, this
practice has nullified a good deal of its work.

The third achievement was to have provided a model which
can influence countries outside Europe, and has indeed,
already done so. In particular, the Organization of American
States decided in 1959 to draft a similar Convention, and the
Constitutions of some new African States have also incorporated similar provisions.

However important these achievements may turn out to be,
it nevertheless remains evident that the world has a long way
to go before we can hope to see nations prepared to agree to
recognize certain minimum, internationally determined, standards of conduct in the field of human rights. Though it may
be easier for individual countries to make progress within their
own frontiers, even with good government and good luck, and
both will doubtless be needed, there is a limit to what institutions, even the best of them, can do. In discussing this problem
of fundamental rights, we have up to now left out of account
two very important practical difficulties which both Governments and citizens are bound to encounter as the field of
human rights is extended, and which cannot be overcome
without the co-operation of the citizen. The first is that,
whether rights are laid down in a constitution or not, their
impact on the citizen is inevitably in the form of a prohibition,
and this fact often determines his reactions from the outset.
For example, we tend to be less conscious of the fact that the
State protects our right to freedom of movement than of the
fact that we must not drive on the right-hand side of the road,
disobey the Highway Code, create an obstruction to traffic,
and so on. Every right that we enjoy is, in practical terms, a
right to do, or say, or enjoy something which is defined in
detailed terms and hedged about with limitations, in consequence of which we are forbidden to enjoy the right except
in these conditions.

The conditions are determined by the State's responsibility for ensuring that all citizens have the same rights and liberties. It is our duty to see that others enjoy the same rights as we do, just as it is their duty to see that we are not prevented from enjoying ours. It is inevitable that this should be so, by virtue of the simple fact that we live in society and not on desert islands. Our rights cannot be isolated from those of others, because everything that we do affects others in one way or another. "A right," says Hobhouse, "is, no doubt, a species of claim. What distinguishes it from other claims is that it is one that it is the duty of everyone to respect, and unless this distinction is admitted there is no reason for the use of the term." Without the corresponding obligation, the whole concept of rights becomes meaningless. It is self-defeating, for example, to say that "I have a right to this watch and you have a right to take it from me."[1]

If every right involves in practice duties and prohibitions, then every extension of freedom through the recognition of new rights also curtails freedom through the imposition of new duties. That is why democracy is perpetually faced with the problem of deciding how to achieve a proper balance between rights and duties. And whatever it decides, its success will, in practice, be determined by the extent to which citizens are prepared to perform conscientiously the duties required of them. A totalitarian State faces a less complex situation. The decision, both on the rights which are to be granted and on the duties which will devolve on the citizen in consequence is the Government's, and the citizen has merely to do as he is told. But in a democracy the people as a whole decide in general terms what are to be their rights and duties. The task of the Government is to find ways of translating these desires into action. It is the Government's responsibility to devise the detailed administrative provisions which are required to give effect to them, which means, in practice,

---

[1] Hobhouse, *The Elements of Social Justice*, p. 36.

deciding what are the duties that the citizen will be required to perform. If the citizen refuses to do his part, then the rights which the duties are designed to enforce will be to that extent ineffective.

The second of the practical difficulties is intellectual rather than moral. In our complex modern civilization it is not always possible for citizens (or indeed for Governments) to know enough about the facts to be able to assess accurately what is likely to be the cost, in terms of duties, of recognizing certain rights. The more politically alert an electorate is, the more it is used to weighing up pros and cons, instead of adopting propagandist slogans without thinking about them, the more it is provided by the Government or the Press with information on which rational conclusions can be based, the more likely it is that its judgment of the facts will be sound. For example, housing is to-day a subject on which the average citizen feels so deeply that he is liable to urge his moral right, without always stopping to think whether what is right is also possible, or at least possible on terms which he would, on reflection, be prepared to accept. When the Conservative Party leaders yielded to a demand from the delegates at the 1950 Conservative Conference to include in their electoral programme an undertaking to construct 300,000 houses a year, many of their opponents accused them of yielding to precisely this kind of irresponsible demand. There is no need for us to discuss here whether this accusation was true or fair. What it is important to note is that many of those who made the demand, like many of those who said it was unreasonable, had clearly made up their minds without giving adequate consideration even to those facts that could, with a little effort, be ascertained.

The more the citizen learns to think of rights in terms of duties, the more he is likely to try to assess possibilities rationally and to make reasonable demands. A Government's task can, therefore, be made more or less difficult according as the citizen is more or less instructed about public affairs, and according as he is more or less ready to put into the common pool at least as much as he is ready to take out. To-day, we have to face the hard fact that much more depends on the citizen than it did in the seventeenth and eighteenth centuries. Most of the fundamental rights that we were fighting for then have now been recognized, in democratic States at least, for long enough to convince us that they constitute only the first steps along the road leading us to the freedom of the human personality. When differences of status, of caste, stood visibly in the way of some, it was natural that men's efforts should be concentrated on the attempt to remove these obstacles to individual freedom and opportunity. But when freedom of thought, of opinion, the right to security of person and property, to equality before the law were the recognized legal and constitutional rights of all citizens, it was realized that the State's responsibility did not end there. It still remained to ensure that citizens were not prevented by social disabilities from enjoying their legal rights. We do not all start life on equal terms. Some of us suffer from ills which are as much a creation of society as an individual inheritance. The action of society as a whole is necessary to overcome such obstacles to the development of human personality as are caused by some kinds of ill-health, by lack of education, poverty or the haunting fear of it. To become effective, fundamental political rights need to be supplemented by social rights. The nineteenth century was conscious of the existence of a social problem. But *laisser-faire* doctrines saw it either as insoluble—part of the nature of things—or as soluble primarily by natural economic processes, by the play of competition. Nineteenth-century reformers were anxious to mitigate the worst effects of social inequality, either by individual charity or by social charity, such as poor relief and elementary health precautions or the provision of rudimentary education. But there was not in the nineteenth century any widespread conviction, as there is in the twentieth, that it is part of the State's duty towards the individual to create the social conditions in which he has the chance of making the best of himself. The responsibility undertaken by the twentieth-century State to ensure a greater measure of social justice or equal opportunity, the policy of levelling-up, as it is sometimes called, has meant a great extension of the citizen's rights. And because, as we have seen, the quality of *rights* depends on the spirit and the letter in which *duties* are accepted, the modern citizen's duties have become equally far-reaching. This relationship between rights and duties has to be worked out afresh all the time, because men's needs and the physical facts are always changing. The citizen has to decide whether his Government is doing everything possible to enforce the rights to which lip-service is being paid, and if not, how it can be persuaded to do more. He has to find ways of ensuring that both he and his compatriots accept their responsibilities as enthusiastically as they claim their rights.

CHAPTER EIGHT

Rights and Duties in a Modern Democracy

IF a nineteenth-century Englishman could return to this earth and compare the position of the citizen to-day with that of the citizen of a century ago, he would certainly not fail to note two striking changes. First, the modern citizen is much more dependent on the State, not only for the essentials of civilized life, but for much of what goes to make up his standard of living; and second, the problem of the relation of rights to duties has become much more complex. The two changes are inevitably closely related. As the minimum standard rises, as the citizen comes to demand more and more from the State, obligations increase commensurately with rights. But the increase is not merely quantitative. It is also qualitative. Our conceptions of what men require from the State in order to lead a full life have moved from the purely physical plane to include the intellectual, the emotional and the psychological. The problems of translating these requirements into practical policies are such that it is becoming less and less possible to find solutions for them in terms of hard and fast rules. At one time, the citizen's rights amounted to little more than the right to be protected from physical assault and from starvation. To-day, the right to be protected from starvation has been extended to include the right to food which is adequate in quality as well as quantity (dried milk for babies, milk and meals for schoolchildren, free or subsidized). The right to be cared for in illness has been extended to include free medical treatment (not only treatment in hospital under the Health Service, but also medical examinations in schools and clinics, school dental and

X-ray services, the provision of special open-air schools for delicate children and of specially equipped schools for the physically handicapped). The right to be protected from destitution has become a comprehensive right to social security (including insurance against unemployment or loss of earnings from industrial injury, public assistance for cases where there is special need, as, for example, where a woman is widowed, or deserted by the family breadwinner, special maternity grants and pensions for the old). The number of available responses to differing individual needs has increased a thousandfold.

It is perhaps in the field of education that the qualitative nature of the changes can be seen most clearly. The implications of the right to education have now come to include a vast network of obligations and permissive services, in addition to the original obligation on the part of the State to provide rudimentary instruction in the elements of reading, writing and arithmetic. The modern State aims at fitting the child intellectually and morally, as well as physically, for a full adult life. There are special schools for both physically and mentally handicapped children, special treatments for the morally handicapped (such as those provided for juvenile delinquents, through the probation service, residential schools or psychological clinics), financial assistance with the expense of education (which may include such things as loans to buy bicycles, free transport to and from school, maintenance grants, in addition to tuition grants). Children who live in a home atmosphere which may be physically or morally harmful may be removed from their parents and the State will then assume the responsibility of finding more suitable homes for them.

All these services—and they are only a fraction of what the State provides to-day—have enormously increased the social and economic opportunities of hundreds of thousands of citizens. They have done so, however, only at the cost of imposing on some citizens a commensurately increased financial burden. The community as a whole is taking on more and more of the responsibility for maintaining a certain minimum standard for all, and over the last century that minimum has been consistently rising. Whether this tendency is conceived of as an extension or as a restriction of the rights of the individual depends very largely on the standpoint of the citizen, on whether he is more conscious of new opportunities or of the price that he has to pay for them. If our nineteenth-century visitor were to read the texts of party-political broadcasts, he would discover that where one party regards certain measures as designed to set men free and to bring society nearer to equality, another regards them as constituting unjustifiable encroachments on individual liberty and as imposing heavy burdens on one section of the community in the exclusive interests of another and to the ultimate disadvantage of society as a whole.

One explanation of these divergent views is that the two sides are assessing differently the importance of the time factor. When a society sets out consciously to change the established relations between different sections of the community, to extend to the community as a whole, the rights previously enjoyed by some, or by only a few, it creates a situation in which time is needed before a new equilibrium can be reached. The immediately perceptible consequence of the introduction of the new policy is that, while one section of the community may be mainly conscious of the existence of new rights, another is mainly, and perhaps exclusively, conscious of the imposition of new duties. It is true that, if the new rights are to be fully effective and to justify their existence, the recipients will also have to accept new obligations, and that the section of the community which is at present only duty-conscious will sooner or later receive benefits. But it takes time for these changes to take place, while the grant of new rights to some and the imposition of new duties on others are both immediate.

It is possible that the stage at which the rights-conscious

become equally conscious of their duties, and the duty-conscious feel that they are receiving commensurate benefits will never be reached. We can never be certain beyond doubt how people will react to new situations. Moreover, if the majority of the citizens become convinced, rightly or wrongly, that the new developments are not producing sufficient benefits to justify themselves, then they may abandon the experiment and return to former habits, or work out some new system. Let us consider for a moment one example, both of increased dependence on the State and of the extension of rights and the imposition of new duties. The introduction of a National Health Service has made the citizen far more dependent on the State. By making the private medical services, which many people relied on previously, so expensive as to be out of reach of all but the wealthier sections of the community, it has, in effect, forced the majority of citizens to participate in the scheme. But whether they do or do not use the services provided by the State, they are compelled to pay for them through taxation. If they do use them, then they are obliged to submit to the conditions laid down, to choose, say, between this or that doctor, or between this or that hospital or treatment, only within the limits and conditions which the State imposes.

Viewed from this angle, the National Health Service consists of a series of obligations. It is true that every citizen has had his say in the matter, in the sense that he voted in a general election either for the party that did or for the one that did not believe in the need to introduce this service in its present form. But most of those who dislike the scheme are more aware of the compulsions which it has brought into their lives than of the fact that their parents had a forty-millionth share in deciding whether or not to have a National Health Service. To those who welcome the scheme, however, it appears in a quite different light. If an unskilled wage-earner has to choose whether what he can save out of, say, £25 to £40 a week is to be devoted to saving for his old age, or for his children's education, or to putting a little by to replace wages lost through illness or unemployment, he is likely to feel far freer if the State takes all the responsibility of dealing with illness in the family off his shoulders, in return for contributions, deducted, along with the rest of his insurance, from his wages. In theory, at least, he has been set free to undertake responsibilities more beneficial to himself and to the community as a whole.

Looked at in this way, increasing dependence on the State is, or should be, counterbalanced by the creation of new opportunities of increasing the welfare of the community. Personal responsibility, says G. D. H. Cole, "has been *limited* in the sense that the State now does a great deal more for the individual than it used to do." This means, not that personal responsibility is being destroyed, but that "it has enabled a great many more people squarely to face their responsibilities, by making these less impossibly burdensome. The modern parent, by and large, does not feel less responsibility for the welfare of his children than his parents or grandparents did: he feels more. There are a great many fewer cases of neglect, of sheer abandonment . . . and this is not only because parents are compelled to behave better, but at least as much because they are given a better chance and a more manageable task."

These, then, are the conflicting points of view. But it is when it comes to interpreting expressions like "enabling" people to face new responsibilities, "giving them a better chance", that the divergencies between the new rights-conscious and the new duty-conscious become most acutely marked. Opponents of the modern minimum standard can quote examples of abuses of the new services, and in particular of the Health Service. They can point to the figures of juvenile delinquency as indicating that the sense of parental and individual responsibility is diminishing, rather than increasing. Supporters can argue that these figures prove nothing, that more delinquency is detected nowadays, or that there are special reasons, such as the fear of nuclear war, to account for them. Both sides can produce facts *ad infinitum* to back up their own contentions.

Our nineteenth-century visitor would probably choose between them no more and no less sensibly than we do. However patiently we collect facts, even if we had the knowledge, industry and single-mindedness of a Karl Marx, to say nothing of his ability to use the resources of the British Museum, we should still be unable to collect enough facts to convince our opponents, and we might not even be able to satisfy ourselves as to where the truth lay. For we are looking at the British scene at a moment when the State has imposed new obligations, but when the hoped-for benefits are still not fully apparent. And so, while some are convinced that they will prove to be well worth the cost, others are far from certain. If increased health, leisure and comfort merely lead to increased attendances at football matches, dog races and bingo sessions, then there will be a net economic loss to the community. People may be happier; the situation may be one which is morally more just. But we shall certainly all be poorer.

The British citizen of to-day who tries to work out what are his rights and duties is faced with the need to find answers to a whole series of questions raised by the introduction of new social and economic opportunities. First, is our conviction that the grant of new rights will be followed by the acceptance of new duties strong enough to justify us in pressing for the maintenance of the new standard? If we decide that, at the present time, we should be justified in paying the cost of maintaining this standard, only if we can ensure that the hoped-for results do, in fact, follow, but that, as things stand at present, there seems little likelihood of that happening, then we must try to answer a further question. Is it our duty to accept the new obligations, together with the further obligation of compelling the beneficiaries (or alternatively educating them to agree voluntarily) to perform the new duties incumbent upon them? If so, how is this to be done, or can it be done at all? Will that not mean increasing still further the citizen's dependence on the State? If we decide that the anticipated social or economic benefit is *not* the only justification for the acceptance of the new responsibilities towards the handicapped sections of the community, we have then to decide on what grounds we either accept or reject them.

It is part of the purpose of this book to suggest the kind of question that the modern citizen is asking, or which is at the back of his mind, but it is no part of its purpose to supply answers. That task is, and must be, the citizen's own responsibility. In so far as he votes for, or supports in any way, one or other of the political parties, he is, in effect, providing an answer. The extent to which it is a conscious answer is a measure of the quality of his citizenship. It is clear that the complex network of contemporary social and economic legislation, while it may be solving some problems, is creating others. To-day, we no longer fear poverty and disease as much as we did in 1850; we fear bad housing and malnutrition less than we did in 1930. But neither in 1850 nor in 1930 was there the anxiety which is felt to-day about problems such as incentives, the right use of controls and subsidies, the relation of welfare to productivity, the function of Trade Unions in the State.

It is impossible in the scope of one chapter to do more than refer briefly to a few of the implications of the rapidly changing relations between citizens of different classes and income groups. But something ought to be said of at least two modern claims to rights, whose relations to duties modern generations have not yet completely worked out. They are the claim to the right to work or maintenance, and to the right to social security, or social welfare. Although these rights are to-day uppermost in the minds of many people and are widely discussed, it is not always easy to discover precisely what those who claim them are asking for and what demands on themselves they are prepared to acknowledge in return.

To begin with, the expression, "the right to work" is, in itself, an example of the way in which claims to rights reflect the dominant preoccupations of an age. Work was for long regarded as the curse of Adam, and as late as the eighteenth century, many Utopias described communities whose most striking feature was that nobody worked. In our own times, Bernard Shaw propounded the theory that in a rationally organized society, we should share equally in the perform- ance of the routine disagreeable tasks (which he assumed would occupy only a few hours a day) and do the interesting things, such as teaching or writing, for the fun of it. It is only with the coming of modern industrialism, with its cyclic economic crises and recurrent periods of widespread unem- ployment, that it has dawned on the average man that work is not an evil to which man was born, but a means of livelihood which sometimes fails him and so causes personal tragedy.

One of the earliest claims to a "right to work" was put forward in France a few years before the revolution of 1848 and the right to work or maintenance was included in the Constitution of that year (Article 8 of the Preamble). British practice has recognized the right to maintenance since the introduction of unemployment insurance in 1911, but it was only in 1943 that the State assumed, implicitly, the responsi- bility for providing men with work. In the White Paper on Employment, the Government recognized that maintaining "a high and stable level of employment" was part of the duty of the State as well as the responsibility of the private employer. The rights to work, to strike, to join a Trade Union, and the right to social security were all specifically mentioned in the Preamble of the 1946 French Constitution and implicitly in that of 1958. They are implicitly recognized to-day by almost all modern democratic States, at least in the form of mea- sures to provide unemployment insurance or assistance, and often in the form of attempts by the State to main- tain full employment and extend the range of the social services.

It may be noted, however, that the political parties which derive the bulk of their support from the working classes, and which are among the most ardent claimants of the right to work, are precisely those which have protested most energetically against the exploitation of the worker and fought for shorter hours of work. The improvements in working conditions during the course of the past century and the growth of support for social reform are evidence of a widespread conviction that society has been providing some workers with too much work and paying them too little for it. The explanation of the apparent contradiction is that, like other rights, the right to work is a statement of principle which is interpreted in practice in the light of different mental reservations and assumptions in the minds of the claimants. To some, it means primarily the duty of the State to pursue a policy which will prevent large-scale unemployment; to others it means the right of the individual to choose the kind of job that he feels himself fitted to do, in the region in which he wants to live, at a wage which he considers adequate, in conditions that he holds to be reasonable. The claimants also assume that by "work", socially or economically useful work is to be understood. Otherwise, the right to work would have been maintained if half of us were digging holes in the road for the other half to fill up. When recipients of poor relief were actually required to perform similarly useless work, there was indignation, particularly in circles which support the claim to a right to work.

Another attitude fairly frequently encountered in England to-day shows in the same way how uncertain is our definition of the right to work. We often hear of strikes declared in protest against dismissals on the score of redundancy. From the economic point of view, this kind of action is not very far removed from demanding the right to dig holes in order to fill them up again. There is no more loss to the community if, say, twenty men out of a hundred are sacked and given unemployment benefit, than if one hundred men slack for twenty per cent of the time in order to keep the extra twenty at work. There might well be an economic gain, for some of the dismissed men would no doubt find more productive employment. It is questionable, too, whether it is morally any more humiliating for a man to feel that society does not need him and is obliged to keep him, than for him to draw his salary for work which could be done equally efficiently without his services. But this attitude to redundancy does not necessarily reflect a reasoned interpretation of what is implied by the right to work. It is more probably the instinctive defence mechanism of an unemployment-haunted generation, which tends, in its fear, to lose sight of the fact that work is a means to an end, and not an end in itself.

The fact that there is no generally agreed definition of the right to work makes it all the easier for confusions and con-tradictions to arise. We need to know the conditions governing the exercise of the right. Does the right to choose one's job mean that a man has the right to refuse to work until he can find a job to suit him? Has he a right to maintenance if he refuses to take a job that the authorities consider suitable, but that he does not? How much maintenance ought he to be entitled to, and for how long, and in return for what obligations on his part? Does the right to choose a job also imply the right to choose to do it as well or as badly as one pleases? How is a "reasonable" wage to be determined, or "reasonable" conditions? What rights to a say in the matter have workers, employers, the Government and the public in general? Should the right to work be interpreted to include, as it often does, the right to strike, and if so, in what circumstances?

Until we can reach some general agreement on questions such as these, the right to work will continue to mean different things to different people. As a beginning, we have to satisfy ourselves on the two practical points which, as we argued at the end of the last chapter, ought always to be present in our minds when we are discussing rights. We must be reasonably convinced that our interpretation of "the right to work" does not leave out of account the obligations which the grant of the right will impose on us. Second, we must ask ourselves whether the facts rule out certain interpretations as impracticable.

A more realistic way of putting these two questions is to ask whether a State to-day can successfully pursue a policy of full employment. The answer is, first, that we do not know how far the facts make it possible, because we do not yet fully understand the economics of unemployment, nor the extent to which, in any given country, international repercussions can render a national policy ineffective. Second, we do not know how far incompatible demands put forward by people with different conceptions of the right to work can also make it ineffective. It may be that full employment can be maintained only on conditions which have not been envisaged and which, on reflection, many of us would not be prepared to accept. For example, to refer again to the problem of redundancy, to interpret the right to work as meaning the right not to be sacked when one's work ceases to be necessary *could* defeat a policy of full employment. By insisting on less efficient methods of production, it could slowly but surely raise the price of British goods until, eventually, we priced ourselves out of our export markets, and so became unable to buy the raw materials, without which full employment could not be maintained. Part of the price of maintaining full employment might, therefore, be the readiness of some people to accept dismissal on the ground of redundancy. This does not necessarily mean accepting anything as drastic as control of labour (in peace-time), but it probably ought to mean the willingness of the "redundant" to be re-trained for jobs in which their services would be more productive, or re-housed in regions which need their labour, and it probably ought to mean also the willingness of the State to provide the necessary facilities.

There are other similar dilemmas that might confront us. Part of the price of maintaining a Welfare State must be our ability and our willingness to provide the personnel required to run the services that we require from it. If there are not enough school-teachers, doctors or nurses, for instance, then the system will break down. The fact that some workers are indispensable can also constitute a threat to the efficient working of the system. For one thing, their indispensability can always be a temptation to them to strike. The right to strike is held by the workers—or by most of them—to be implicit in the right to work, since the primary aim of a strike is to enforce respect for conditions that the strikers feel to be inherent in the right to work, as they define it. Clearly, however, strikes in essential industries could paralyse production and impoverish a nation to such an extent that it would be impossible to maintain the very conditions which the strike was intended to enforce. However morally justifiable a strike may be, there are circumstances in which it is bound to defeat its own ends, if it endangers the policy of full employment, on whose success the standard of living ultimately depends.

All these examples really add up to the following conclusion. As soon as we begin to analyse what we mean by the right to work, we discover that it is impossible to divorce the consideration of what is right from what is possible. When we claim the right to work, what we are doing is making a whole series of claims to particular rights which seem to us to be implicit in the definition. Each of them has to be judged in practice, however, on its merits in the light of the particular set of circumstances in which it is claimed, before we can decide how far, on balance, its recognition is possible, in that form, at that time and in that place, and at a cost that we are prepared to pay then and there. In making this estimate, we have also got to take into account moral as well as economic considerations and try to decide which is to have priority, if they are incompatible.

All this does not mean that no purpose is served by declaring our belief in the principle of the right to work. It may, or may not, be a good thing to draw attention to the need to value work properly by including the right to work in a constitution. As we have seen, however, to do so is really only to state an intention, to express an ideal. That may be, in itself, morally useful, as an inspiration and a touchstone, but it is only a first step. As soon as the ideal has to be translated into concrete measures of enforcement, the difficulties come thick and fast. The citizen must be careful to avoid two pitfalls. He must not confuse the will for the deed and be satisfied with a mere paper declaration of principle. Nor must he necessarily conclude that because all the complicated issues which this right, like any other, is bound to raise in practice, make its reduction to a simple formula unrealistic, it would be better to abandon the ideal. The fact that we mean different things by the right to work need not blind us to the validity of the sentiments that the phrase seeks to express. It is essentially the cry of the Levellers of the seventeenth century: "The poorest he that is in England hath a life to live as the greatest he". It is the affirmation of the inherent right of the individual to the dignity and self-respect that come from feeling that he is needed, that what he has to contribute to the community counts. The practical ways of giving expression to the principle will vary with circumstances, and from time to time and country to country. But a State which ignored the aspiration would soon find itself as much out of touch with reality as it would if it assumed too easily that the road to its fulfilment was a clearly marked highway.

Up to now, we have discussed the right to work, only in terms of its possible internal contradictions. But what we decide regarding the right to work will inevitably affect what we decide regarding other rights. If we believe at one and the same time that we ought not to be asked to work more than forty hours a week and that we ought to have access to social services which we can see our way to pay for only if we work for fifty hours a week, then one or other of our claims will have to be modified. Before our analysis of any right is complete, it will have to take into account the cost, not merely in terms of the duties that will be called for within the same sphere, but also of the sacrifices of alternative rights that may be involved.

The right to social welfare is inextricably bound up with the right to work, by virtue of the simple fact that all the material benefits that we get from society are, in the long run, paid for by the work of society. How much work and how much welfare? These are questions that cannot be answered independently of each other. The redistribution of wealth which the new social standards have inevitably entailed has made it necessary for us to think many things out afresh. We have to decide, for example, what we mean, at this stage of the twentieth century, by the right to property. Locke's views on property have already been mentioned. Others could be quoted, much nearer our own time, which would appear to many British citizens to be much more out of harmony with modern conceptions. Except for a handful of convinced Communists, whose attitude on this point has never been clearly defined, all political parties to-day would uphold the right of the individual to possess property, but on conditions which differ considerably to-day from those that were considered normal, even a couple of generations ago. To-day, there are not many extreme Conservatives who would support their belief in the right to property on the grounds put forward in 1912 by Lord Hugh Cecil. "The simple consideration," he wrote, "that it is wrong to inflict an injury upon any man suffices to constitute a right to private property where such property already exists."[1] Village labourers or suburban householders might perhaps be excused for reflecting with some bitterness that Lord Hugh Cecil could count himself fortunate that plenty of Cecil property did already exist and had been in existence for some considerable time, and that no member of the Salisbury family was likely to have to live in a tied cottage or pay interest to a building society for twenty

---

[1] *Conservatism* (Home University Library, 1912), p. 120.

years in order to keep a roof over his head. In 1801, Harriet Martineau—and she spoke for many of her compatriots—could regard the privilege of wealth and the benevolence of charity as equally natural. To-day, many more of her compatriots would agree with Shaw that "those who like playing the good Samaritan should remember that you cannot have good Samaritans without thieves."[1]

Nor is it only the attitude to property as a right that has changed with the increasing emphasis on social rights. The practical possibilities of owning property may be restricted by the need to pay for the new services. If society does not create sufficient new wealth to enable it to foot the bill, and so far it has not been able to do so, then it is obliged to take more of the income of the wealthy, in the form of taxes. This may well make it impossible for many property owners to continue to hold property on the same scale as before, because they can no longer maintain it. Not only, therefore, do the new rights modify conceptions of existing rights, but they may be actually incompatible with them. To quote merely one or two examples: the right of women to economic as well as political equality is bound eventually, either to modify existing conceptions of the duties of husbands, or of both husbands and the State, towards children, or, alternatively to restrict the rights of children, for the simple reason that women cannot be in two places at once and some of them, if given the choice, will choose to work outside the home. The right of children to receive education up to the age of sixteen, or rather the duty to remain at school, which is the form in which that particular right is expressed, restricts their right to work. If the right to retire were fixed for men and women at sixty and fifty-five respectively, instead of, as now, at sixty-five and sixty, these benefits would have to be paid for by increased production on the part of those who had not yet reached that age. The lower

---

[1] *The Intelligent Woman's Guide to Socialism and Capitalism* (Constable, 1928), p. 96.

the retiring age, the more work is available for the younger generation, but the greater the proportion of what they earn will go to maintain the non-productive. The more we all become owners of the nation's wealth, the less choice some of us have, as individuals, in the spending of it. For public ownership means planning, and planning means controls. I now have one forty-millionth of a say in the running of the nationalized transport service, whereas I had none at all in its running as a private industry. But then I could choose whether I would go to a number of places by bus or by train. When the industry has been replanned, I may expect to derive certain advantages, both economic and moral, from the fact of public ownership, but I shall almost certainly lose in return some of my right to choose.

The implications of social security, or social welfare, have to be considered in this context as well as in that of social justice and fair shares for all. In economic terms, if the new services cost more than can be provided by the new productive resources which they make available, then the community will have to pay for them, now or later, by sacrificing something else.

If the community values what it is receiving more highly than what it is sacrificing, then the price may not be felt to be too high. It is possible for a society to decide that the increase in the individual dignity and social well-being of the classes to whom the new services are available is well worth the sacrifice of some material resources by the better-off sections, and all the more so if there is a general conviction that the sacrifice will be merely a transitional phenomenon and that eventually most of us will be better off. The citizen may have to decide, however, how long he is prepared to give the new system a trial, before he concludes that the increased production is not going to be forthcoming, and what he is to do if he does come to that conclusion.

We have already referred to this aspect of the problem in discussing the changes in rights and duties consequent upon the introduction of the National Health Service. But it really goes much deeper than that. It is not merely a question of convincing those who at present regard it as a burden that they stand to gain in the long run, or of convincing those who regard it as a benefit that it is their duty not to exact too high a price from the others by abusing their new rights. In the long run, the beneficiaries will also be the poorer, if there is no clear understanding of the nature of the duties that are implicit in the exercise of the rights. In the nineteenth century, it was possible for the rich to pay for increased benefits to the poor. But at the rate at which social reforms have been carried out during the course of the past generation, this cannot go on very long unless total wealth also increases very rapidly. In Great Britain and many European countries, economic and social changes and two world wars have contributed to increase taxation to such an extent that social services can no longer depend on this source of revenue. The proceeds of taxation of the wealthy pay a progressively smaller proportion of the bill with every year that passes. Henceforth, unless present trends are reversed, the poor will be paying for the poorer, as well as for themselves. It was Bernard Shaw who pointed out in *The Intelligent Woman's Guide* that in a household of two which employs a staff of nine there are not two people looked after by nine, but eleven.

This means two things. It means, first, that the citizen is vitally interested in keeping the bill as low as is consistent with the maintenance of a proper level of efficiency and service. This does not mean merely complaining about administrative extravagance; it also means avoiding contributing by his own actions to wasteful abuse of the services provided. If several million members of the Health Service throw away their medicine bottles, or obtain unnecessary prescriptions for aspirin, then, although they may not realize it, it is largely they themselves who are paying for both the aspirins and the luxury of being wasteful. It means, secondly, that, until the nation's total resources can be increased, the maintenance of some social services will result in our having to do without other forms of welfare. We cannot have our cake and eat it.

For the citizen to decide what standard of social welfare he has a right to, without at the same time trying to take into account who is paying for it and how, is, therefore, merely to indulge in Utopian fantasy. The choice is rather between so much education, so many pensions and allowances, so much medical treatment, on the one hand, and so many cinemas, television sets, holidays, and even perhaps houses, hotels or roads, on the other. It is a choice between working harder and more efficiently in order to produce more wealth, which may involve accepting all sorts of restrictions and discomforts, such as shift work, longer hours, narrowing of differentials, being dismissed for redundancy, having uneconomic factories and mines closed down . . .; or choosing to put off paying in the hope that conditions will improve; or reducing the benefits to a level at which we can afford to pay for them without putting ourselves out too much; or instituting drastic economies in management in the hope that greater efficiency will reduce the cost to a more manageable total.

It is possible to dispute every one of the above points, on the ground that they do not represent true estimates of the facts. There are, no doubt, economists who would maintain indignantly that what we have been talking about are not political, but economic facts, and that, if politics cannot really be called a science, economics can, and economic facts can be determined with scientific accuracy. That may or may not be so. But it is relevant to reply that on all these issues, and indeed on any others on which the political parties disagree, each side can produce a batch of reputable economists to back up its case. We shall, therefore, maintain the opinion that the decision is really a political one and refuse to enter into any discussion on the merits of the relative claims of applied economics and politics to be described as sciences. All that has been said earlier indicates that what the Government will act on will be what the majority of us believe to be the most relevant facts.

The citizen has, therefore, three courses of action open to him. He can decide to accept the interpretation of the facts arrived at by one of the political parties, and leave the party leaders to fight his battles for him. Or he can decide that what he wants or believes to be right *must* be possible, and act on that assumption. Or he can try to work out for himself what obligations he ought to accept, in order to contribute either to lessening the cost of the services that he believes ought to be available, or to increasing the wealth of the community in general. In what is called the welfare State, the level of social and economic opportunity is bound to be predominantly determined by the price that the citizen is prepared to pay for the rights that he claims. When the rights guaranteed by the State were few, the duties of the citizen were correspondingly few and he was often far more conscious of his obligations to his employer, his church and his family than he was of his obligations to the State. To-day, he has come to depend on the State for so much, that families, employers and workers are equally conscious of the intervention of the State in almost every department of their lives. If that dependence is not to transform the citizen into a passive beneficiary, or even a victim of the State, he will have to play an active part in ensuring that the duties which will make possible the granting of the rights that he considers essential are effectively performed. That does not mean that he will have to become an active politician. It does mean that, within the sphere of his own interests, being a good citizen may demand more of him than it has done in the past and that if he refuses to accept the new responsibilities, he will be helping to justify the fears of those who hold that the modern State does too much for the citizen. It does not mean either that those who claimed and fought for rights in the past, without regard to cost, were wrong. It means rather that the emphasis has changed. To-day, it is no longer as necessary as it was to ask *what* our fundamental rights are. Most of them are now generally recognized in democratic States and others are within our grasp. Nowadays, we tend to ask rather what we want, or ought, to pay for rights and whether we want to pay the price all at once, or in instalments. In other words, in a democracy we can insist that the State shall guarantee whatever rights we claim. But since we cannot manipulate the facts in order to obtain them on exactly the terms that we would prefer, we look at the problem in a more administrative and practical way and ask ourselves how we can best get what we want, what is the most economical method, in terms of time, effort and sacrifice.

Much of the assessment of the cost of rights in terms of personal effort or sacrifice is unconscious and much of it is, inevitably, made after decisions have been taken and when it may be difficult, if not impossible, to go back on them. Perhaps the most agonizing of the dilemmas that the citizen has been called upon to face in trying to make provisional estimates of where his duty lies is that created by the threat of war. War has always brought personal suffering and loss, but in earlier times, it did not involve the moral dilemmas that the threat of war does to-day. Before the advent of democracy and compulsory military service, armies were mainly composed of volunteers or mercenaries. They were small, and the impact of war on the life of the community was, by modern standards, infinitesimal. Now that wars are made, not by absolute monarchs, but by democratic States with representative Governments, the citizen is ultimately responsible for the decision whether or not to fight. And because modern war may become a nuclear war, his children and their children will be vitally affected by his decision.

It is worth while discussing this problem of the danger of nuclear war in somewhat greater detail, because it is not only the most difficult moral dilemma with which the citizen is likely to be faced but also one which many young people to-day find peculiarly agonizing. The democratic thesis is that, although the danger of such an eventuality exists, it is a danger that it is one of the primary aims of a democracy to avoid. But the difficulties and deadlocks in the field of foreign policy that have been discussed in Chapter Five are such that many people feel insecure and helpless. Some are critical of the policies of Western democracies. Some feel that, in reality, they have no policy, since the only effective defence in a nuclear war is that of the United States.

The result has been that citizens in many countries have reacted against this feeling of individual and even national helplessness and have, in effect, adopted one of three attitudes. Some contract out and leave their party leaders to do the thinking for them, others try as best they can to work out the pros and cons of different policies—theories of relative or catalytic deterrence and of disengagement; possibilities of limiting or controlling the use of nuclear weapons, either through general disarmament or through bi-lateral agreements; possibilities of acquiring for the European powers some say in the use of nuclear weapons, either through a closer co-ordination of strategy, or through the development of a European deterrent, or through the acceptance by the United States of shared responsibility, in NATO, for the decision to use nuclear weapons; the possibility of bringing pressure to bear on the United States to agree to some shared control, by the development of a national independent deterrent force, such as the French *force de frappe*. Others, in the face of endless and abortive disarmament conferences, disagreements in NATO and in Europe, fear the proliferation of nuclear weapons and the consequent spread of the danger of an accidental or irresponsible triggering-off of a nuclear war by some smaller power, and have therefore decided either that this is not the right road, or that it is not a road which allows the citizen any real say in vital decisions. They have, therefore, adopted either a policy of neutralism, as most of the Afro-Asian countries have done, or have decided that the only way out of the deadlock is for some Great Power to have the courage to give a lead and renounce, unilaterally if necessary, the use of nuclear weapons altogether.

A few, like the Quakers, who adopt the position of out-and-out pacifism, have concentrated wholly on the moral problem, leaving the political consequences to take care of themselves, or in the hands of God, according to their religious beliefs. This position is, of course, admissible in a democratic society that believes in the right to freedom of opinion and religious belief. It is a minority view which a democracy would be unwise to refuse to recognize, if it is anxious to preserve the principle of consent. In both the 1914 and 1939 wars, British Governments recognized the citizen's right to conscientious objection. France refused then, and continued up to 1963, to refuse to recognize this right, on the ground that national defence was one of the essential duties of citizenship. But even more than neutralism, conscientious objection constitutes a form of contracting out. It really provides no solution to the dilemma of the student of political science, who believes that the citizen should share responsibility for the political decisions that have to be taken by Governments.

A policy of unilateral nuclear disarmament can, of course, be based on pacifism. But it need not be and often is not. Its attraction, particularly to many young people, is precisely that it can be stated in a form that does not appear to constitute contracting out. Demonstrators who sit down in Trafalgar Square, or in front of Embassies, or who walk from London to Aldermaston, believe that this is a positive action by the citizen which will in some way contribute to bringing safety from the nuclear danger nearer. They do not always give very clear or articulate explanations of *how* this causal connection is established. But there is no doubt that *they* feel it. To others, who cannot make the assumption that demonstrations such as these are likely to achieve these results, their arguments are both unconvincing and dangerous. For they can become easy substitutes for the slower, more difficult, but more realistic task of trying to get nations to agree little by little on how to settle their differences peaceably.

In the last resort, what is important is that citizens should at least make the effort to answer the questions about how to save the world from war—from conventional as well as nuclear war, for both are lethal—to the satisfaction of their own consciences, and that these should as far as possible be respected by Governments. It is difficult, however, to see why this respect should be accorded to citizens who attempt to bring pressure on Governments by illegal means, when legal means exist. The weapon of illegality is surely a bad one, because it is one that attempts to gain a specific good, by using weapons that threaten society with a general evil—namely disrespect for democratically determined institutions.

CHAPTER NINE

Liberty and Equality

WE have defined the purpose of rights as being to enable men
to live, to enjoy life and to develop to the full the potentialities of their individual personalities. Rights, then, are a
means to an end. That end, though it may differ in many ways
for different individuals, may be summed up in the one word,
liberty. Men want to be free to live their own lives in their
own way, and the attainment of that ambition constitutes
liberty, or freedom. The rights and duties that we have been
discussing in the last two chapters can therefore be considered
adequate, only if they succeed in providing the citizen with
an environment in which he is truly free to be himself. What
we must now ask ourselves is how we are to know whether
that end has been achieved. Can we discover any general
standards by which we can measure the degree to which
liberty exists?

Before we go on to consider some of the ways in which this
question has been answered, there are two points of definition
on which it is necessary to be quite clear in our minds. Liberty,
as we have defined it, means moral freedom, riot absence of
restraints on our freedom of action. Clearly, as we have seen,
men who live in society cannot be free from all restraints. If
they were, the result would be, not liberty, but licence,
anarchy, chaos. Restraints are necessary in the interests of
order and of the harmonization, in so far as that is possible,
of our different conceptions of liberty. As Hobhouse has put
it: "The liberty of each . . . must, on the principle of the
common good, be limited by the rights of all; . . . in general,
my rights are my liberties; and in protecting my rights, the

community secures my liberties." "The system of rights is the system of harmonized liberties." We might express this differently, by saying that, in the ideal State, the individual's personal liberties (or rights) and restraints (or duties) would be so harmonized that we achieved the ideal of liberty, that is, a condition in which every individual enjoyed the maximum freedom to do as he pleased, compatible with the right of others to the same degree of freedom.

On this definition, liberty is moral freedom, and equality is essential to it, for without equality, the price of liberty for me might be the denial of liberty for you. That this is a commonly held view is suggested by the frequent association of liberty and equality in claims to fundamental rights. But the two have not always and everywhere been claimed with equal fervour. On the whole, Anglo-Saxons have seemed to place more emphasis on liberty, while the French have always sought, first and foremost, to secure recognition of the principle of equality. It is possible to explain this difference of emphasis as the result of different political evolutions or of different national characteristics. It is also possible to explain it by saying that, in reality, one or the other has to be chosen, because the two demands are really incompatible, that, as Lord Acton said, "the passion for equality makes vain the hope of freedom."

Whether equality is a condition of liberty or is in reality incompatible with it is a question that we shall obviously have to answer for ourselves before we try to decide how far systems of rights and duties do or do not succeed in creating liberty, and the answer we give is bound to affect our whole way of looking at the problem. We may not be able to come down definitely on one side or the other. But if we think that at least a considerable measure of equality is necessary to the attainment of liberty, then the importance that we attach to equality, what we think is justified by it, will constitute to some extent criteria by which we judge the quality of liberty. If, on the other hand, we feel that equality is irrelevant to, or even incompatible with the attainment of liberty, we shall have to seek our criteria elsewhere.

The second point on which we must be clear is that the standards by which we judge whether we have liberty or not, or whether we are at least on the right road, will be quite different according as we do or do not believe that the means to an end are part of the end, and must be judged by the same standards of value. It is one of the assumptions of democracy that the means cannot be divorced from the end. Or to put it in simple, everyday language, democracies assume that, in so far as it is humanly possible, they must not do evil that good may come. Freedom, therefore, is something that can be created only by free men. The road to liberty must itself be freely chosen and the journey undertaken without compulsion. On the democratic thesis, the citizen himself decides both what constitutes his freedom (or his happiness or whatever we choose to describe as the purpose of politics), and also the means which he will employ to achieve his end. These means are themselves judged by the same standard of value as the ends.

This association of means and ends follows quite naturally from the central assumption of democracy, which is, as we have seen throughout this book, that all our political standards of value are determined, in the last resort, by the individual. We have no objective criterion of what is good, right, best, or just. All we have is the sum of individual opinions, which we have to interpret as best we can, through the medium of political institutions. In discussing liberty, rights or duties, we therefore assume that only the individual himself is competent to take decisions on matters so vital to him. It is his decision that determines the rights and duties through which, in his view, liberty can best be achieved. And it is again his decision which determines how far individual freedom of action has to be restrained, in the interests of the freedom of all. Every step of the road is taken only with the consent of, and under the direction of, the body of citizens.

Now, these two assumptions, namely, that the individual is the most competent person to decide what he means by liberty and how best to seek it, and that the way in which it is sought will inevitably affect our conception of what we are seeking, are not universally accepted. It is possible to hold that liberty is not the supreme good, or to define it in such a way that its achievement does not depend on the recognition of systems of individual rights and concomitant duties, such as we have discussed. Liberty, in the sense in which Marxists (for instance) understand it, means the freeing of an oppressed class from economic exploitation. It can best be achieved through the action of an enlightened minority, able to establish itself as a Government, with dictatorial powers. If these powers are used to redistribute the material benefits which some have enjoyed at the expense of others, they will re-create the necessary conditions of liberty. Only then will men be free. Only then will it be possible for the State, which restricts individual freedom of action, to wither away.

The Marxist thesis, then, denies the possibility of liberty in the absence of the conditions of economic equality which alone make it possible, and it asserts that economic equality can only be achieved through revolution and dictatorship. Liberty is something which is found at the end of the road, a road along which the mass of citizens are led by a minority of their fellows, who decide the rate of advance and the conditions in which the march shall be made. It is something which is created for men by external conditions, not something which they can possess only if they learn at the same time to have free minds. On the democratic thesis, liberty is something much more like Christian's journey from the City of Destruction to Mount Zion. He set off, we remember, to "go up directly" to a "shining light", which lay some distance ahead. From the outset, his route proved to be neither simple nor direct, and both before and after he had passed the wicket-gate and received his instructions, he encountered obstacles, missed his way and was misled by bad advice. It was a journey on which he set out alone, and it was his own individual effort to keep to the right path, despite the many obstacles he encountered, that led to his ultimate safe arrival.

There is no need to labour the comparison.Throughout this book, it is the democratic thesis of the primacy of the individual that has been adopted. On this assumption, liberty means moral freedom and the judge, both as to the right way to attain it and as to the extent to which it has been attained, is and must remain the individual citizen.

What we are trying to discover is whether there is some general standard by which the average citizen can measure the conduct of Governments or of his fellow citizens. In the last two chapters we were discussing some of the particular standards of measurement. It is possible to argue that no society in which certain fundamental rights are not recognized can be a free society. It is possible, similarly, to argue that certain duties ought not to be required of free citizens. But the average citizen has not the time, nor is he usually sufficiently actively interested in politics, to try to work out the relation of specific rights and duties to the general purpose of the society in which he lives. In most democratic societies, the basic, fundamental rights, such as free speech and freedom of conscience, do constitute the touchstones by which citizens judge of the democratic intentions of Governments. But these are only *minimum* rights. In recognizing them, a Government has not fulfilled its whole duty. What we want to know is something much more positive. We want to know whether we have a right to demand *more* than we are getting, whether the quality of the rights that we enjoy is such as to give us real moral freedom. If it is not, we want to know what, in general, the State can do for us that it is not doing.

In the nineteenth century, John Stuart Mill tried to answer this question, in what has since become a classic definition of liberty. In his view, and it was the accepted attitude of the age, the individual ought to be left as free as possible from interference with his personal freedom of action. He therefore justified State interference on two grounds only. "The individual," he said, "is not accountable to society for his actions, in so far as these concern the interests of no person but himself. Advice, instruction, persuasion and avoidance by other people if thought necessary by them for their own good, are the only measures by which society can justifiably express its dislike or disapprobation of his conduct. Secondly, that for such actions as are prejudicial to the interests of others, the individual is accountable, and may be subjected either to social or to legal punishment, if society is of opinion that the one or the other is requisite for its protection." Mill did not argue that the State was *bound* to interfere, even then. There would be cases where interference would be undesirable, as, for example, when one individual, by succeeding in an overcrowded profession, inadvertently injures the prospects of another. Suffering of this kind would be, he thought, inevitable in any society. There were also cases in which intervention would be inexpedient because it would be ineffective. Restrictions on free trade were "wrong solely because they do not really produce the results which it is desired to produce by them." One of the restrictions that he considered objectionable was that on the sale of poisons. It opened up, he thought, the whole question of "how far liberty may legitimately be invaded for the prevention of crime, or of accident." He thought that individuals ought, in their own interest, to be made aware of danger, and so had a right to be warned, but that they ought not to be forcibly prevented from exposing themselves to danger, if they wished to do so. At this point, their actions came into the category of "self-regarding misconduct". Drunkenness, for example, was not in his view a subject for legislative interference, except when the individual under the influence of drink had been guilty of an act of intolerance towards others.

The modern student, reading Mill's essay, is left with the feeling that, as with so many of the political principles that have been discussed in this book, he can accept the general definitions, but not always their application. It is only when Mill comes down to practical examples that we see how differently the nineteenth and the twentieth centuries look at the individual, and how much less of what we see we are prepared, in the twentieth century, to take for granted, as natural or inevitable. There are two significant differences between Mill's attitude to the problem and the one most commonly accepted to-day. Whereas to-day the freedom of the individual is something that is in great part the creation of the State, for Mill it was something obtained, in the main, by the State's decision to leave the individual alone. It is true that Mill took a less negative view than many of his contemporaries. He did at least envisage cases where it might be necessary for the State to interfere, in order to help people who might not be able to help themselves—for example, by paying for their education, if they were unable to pay for it themselves. Indeed, he believed that education ought to be made compulsory, although he did not think that the State ought to direct education. That, he said, would be "a mere contrivance for moulding people to be exactly like one another." In general, however, he assumed, like most of his contemporaries, that if the State did not prevent citizens from doing something, they had the power to do it. He took it for granted that some were rich and others poor and he realized that the latter were at a disadvantage compared with the former, but he did not regard the State as a positive force, capable of redressing the balance to some extent, and under an obligation to try to do so. Mill's contemporaries would no doubt have accepted as true, not to say obvious, the remark on equality of opportunity made by Bernard Shaw in his *Intelligent Woman's Guide to Socialism and Capitalism.* "Give your son a fountain-pen and a ream of paper," he wrote, "and tell him that he now has an equal opportunity with me of writing plays, and see what he will say to you." It is a measure of the extent to which our conceptions of liberty have changed that Shaw knew how we should answer this challenge. In the twentieth century, the majority of citizens in democratic countries believe that we ought to give everybody's sons, together with the ream of paper and the pen, as much of Bernard Shaw's intellectual opportunities as can be provided by a State education, and a standard of health and nutrition that will enable him to benefit from it. We do not expect to turn out a series of Bernard Shaws. But we do aim at giving those who might want to write plays, or build bridges or become engine drivers or Prime Ministers, enough experience in handling the necessary tools to enable them to make up their minds for themselves whether they want to go on from there to learn the job.

Like his contemporaries, Mill underestimated the extent to which other kinds of interference as well as State interference can restrict liberty. He did not conceive of the State as restricting one kind of liberty in order to protect another, which the individual might not be able to protect for himself. A measure like the Catering Wages Act interferes with the freedom of workers and employers to negotiate terms of employment between themselves. But if it compels some employers to give to some workers better conditions than they could have obtained for themselves, then the latter might feel that the State had increased their freedom. Mill did realize that there were instances where the freedom of certain sections of the community (and he specifically mentions employers) might legitimately be restricted, to ensure that workers were protected from dangerous machinery, for instance, or to ensure that the community was protected by the establishment of proper sanitation. He clearly regarded interference of this kind as exceptional, however, holding, as a general rule, that voluntary actions were more valuable than actions done under compulsion.

Where Mill's approach differs, too, from that of the twentieth century is in its optimism regarding the progress of human nature. His distinction between self- and other-regarding actions would be workable only in a society in which everyone was as rational and tolerant as he was himself. He saw quite clearly that things were not so in the real world and he quoted at some length, and with considerable indignation, instances where it would be difficult to apply his principle owing to the intolerance of certain sections of opinion. He realized that Sabbatarians and teetotallers did not merely want to keep Sunday in their way, or to refuse to drink intoxicating drinks, but also to force others who did not share their views to adopt their practice. He objected to this kind of intolerance and expressed very firmly his conviction that it was wrong to force people to do what *you* believed to be right, against their own convictions. He could have added a host of other examples; opposition to blood sports, to vivisection, to vaccination, to birth control, all undoubtedly come within Mill's category of self-regarding opinions or actions. Unfortunately, the holders of the opinions refuse to regard them in this light. Mill assumed that they would learn to know better and that education would help them to be rational and tolerant. In the twentieth century, we are less optimistic about the prospects of any rapid increase in common sense, and we are certainly less convinced of the power of education to spread tolerance. Modern democracies have had to accept the consensus of opinion as the criterion of self-regarding actions. The norm in this, as in other matters, is what the majority believes, or is prepared to accept. The extent to which the majority is prepared to be tolerant determines the degree of freedom extended to cranks to indulge in their eccentricities.

Modern democratic practice is, thus, at the same time more and less optimistic than Mill. It has a higher estimate of the potentialities of human nature, in that it seeks through State action to free man from a whole range of disabilities which are held to prevent him from enjoying full freedom. It has a lower estimate of men's capacity to learn quickly to undertake certain responsibilities themselves. Mill really thought that once the State decided that education must be compulsory, most parents would carry out their obligations, their "sacred duties", as he called them. He would doubtless be horrified if he could learn of the thousands of other sacred or profane duties that the modern parent and citizen is obliged by the State to perform.

At this point it may well be asked whether we are really talking about liberty at all, or about equality of opportunity as a prerequisite for the enjoyment of liberty. Does what has just been said mean that, whatever may be said about theories, twentieth century practice has assumed that equality is a condition of liberty and not incompatible with it?

Here again we must be careful of our terminology, for the right to equality has often been stated ambiguously, and different claimants have understood different things by it. Equality, for the French revolutionaries, really meant equality before the law, the same law for all and no privileged classes or individuals exempt from its provisions. Until very recent times, equality in Great Britain, in so far as it was claimed as a right, meant equal rights for all to claim the protection of the law of the land and to be judged by the same law. It meant, too, an equal right to the fundamental liberties implied in citizenship; the right to speak one's mind freely, belong to societies or churches, vote without fear of intimidation. It did not imply any right to economic equality. It did not always imply the posssibility of enforcing the legal rights. In a number of cases, individuals were (and sometimes still are) unable to do so because they could not pay the high legal fees that enforcement would involve. In America, on the other hand, equality has usually been interpreted to mean the right to economic opportunity, the absence of any bar to individual achievement on grounds of inherited or class privilege. Opponents of the right to equality have sometimes rejected it on the ground that what its supporters were hankering after was not equality, but identity or uniformity. Others have

taken the claim to imply a belief that, if given equal opportunities, we should all turn out to be equally intelligent.
Others, again, have taken it to mean that none of us ought to
have more property than his neighbour; or, more usually, that
none of us ought to have any property at all, that property
ought to be held in common; or, as the French revolutionaries
thought, that society ought to decide how much property
we ought to possess.

    In the minds of many, the struggle for equality was essen-
tially bound up with the struggle to control or to eliminate
private property. Rousseau began his essay on the origins of
inequality with the affirmation that: "The first man who took
it into his head to put a fence round a piece of land and say,
'This is mine', and who found people simple enough to believe
him, was the real founder of civil society." And he went on:
"What crimes, wars, murders, wretchedness and horror the
human race might have been spared, if only someone had
torn up the stakes or filled in the ditch and cried out to his
neighbours: 'Do not listen to this impostor; you are lost if you
forget that the fruits of the earth belong to all and that the
earth itself belongs to none!' " This is one line of argument.
But it has had as many opponents as supporters. For the concept of property is one that exemplifies, perhaps more than
any other, the difficulty of harmonizing equality and liberty.
The possession of property has been claimed as a fundamental
right without which the individual is unable to realize his
personality to the full; it has been claimed as a just reward for
the individual's own labour, or on the ground that the owner
used it in the service of the public. Yet the possession of
property has meant in practice the creation of inequality and
its perpetuation through inheritance. Throughout the
eighteenth and nineteenth centuries, protests by individuals
and groups against the prevailing political inequality and
economic oppression frequently included protests against
private property. Not only did hundreds of Utopias describe
imaginary communities in which property no longer existed,

but a number of Utopian or communistic communities were actually established, in which either all property was held in common, or there was more or less rigid equality of wages, of profits or of private possessions, where these were allowed. In the nineteenth century, the British co-operator, Robert Owen, and the followers of the French Socialist, Fourier, both set up communities of this kind, and a number of others were established, inspired by their ideas. The French Socialist, Etienne Cabet, founded a colony in America, which he called Icaria, whose principles were, in his own words, "communist fraternity, equality and liberty." "In our society," he wrote, "there is no opulence, but also no poverty. . . . We enjoy the produce in common, according to the needs of each, on the principle of fraternity and equality, with no special privileges for anyone. We have the sovereignty of the people in practice, democracy in principle, liberty in application and an open door to all peaceful reforms."

Icarian communities succeeded each other for nearly fifty years. Like all the other attempts, they, too, broke down. Most of them failed essentially for the same reason. It proved impossible in practice either to suppress private property (or the desire for it) or to secure agreement on where to draw the line deciding how much private property there was to be. When Cabet left his community for a time, the Icarians promptly stopped working for the community, seized plots of land for themselves, just as Rousseau's primitive man had done, and proceeded to look after their own interests. Even while the system was functioning under the personal direction of the leader, he had to deal with constant disputes and attempts to evade the obligation to give up all private property.[1]

Now, these isolated experiments do not, of themselves, provide sufficient evidence that the ideal of equality is a Utopian dream and that human nature will never change. They were small-scale experiments carried out in difficult

---

[1] The agricultural communities established in Israel, too, appear to have become less communistic.

conditions, often by people with little experience of, and less aptitude for, community life. Many of them were based on austere religious principles; their original principles were often watered down by the influx of new members, or of refugees without the enthusiasm of the founders. But the experiments do provide pointers to a possible way of reconciling what have so far been put forward as diametrically opposed points of view. If we look more closely at the quotation from Lord Acton on p. 199, we note that what he found incompatible with liberty was not equality, but "*the passion for equality*". What seems to have rendered so many of these equalitarian communities unworkable was that equality came to be regarded not so much as an aid to liberty as an end in itself. The pioneers were so busy working out their shares and seeing that their neighbours were not getting more than they had a right to, that they lost sight of liberty.

If, then, the principle of equality is too rigidly interpreted, if more attention is paid to mathematically or materially equal shares than to the purpose of increasing freedom, if equality becomes a passion instead of an instrument, then liberty may be diminished by equalitarian measures. The right to equality ought not to imply a right to identical treatment. The modern doctrine of equality of opportunity is based on the refusal to accept the conclusion, so readily accepted by the nineteenth century, that, given a ream of paper and a pen, genius will out. It recognizes, as the Marxist analysis did, that men are conditioned by their environment and that merely to remove legal restrictions is only the first step on the road to freedom. It still remains to persuade the slave who has grown up in his chains, knowing nothing else, not only that he *can* throw them off, but that the effort is worth while. And it still remains to help him to get used to freedom. When people argued that it was not worth while rehousing slum dwellers because they would only keep coal in the bath, they were accepting the fact of conditioning, but drawing exactly the opposite conclusions from those who argued in favour of equality of opportunity. The reply of the latter was that we could not know what people would *normally* do with their coal until everybody had an equal opportunity to get used to having a coal cellar to keep it in.

By equality of opportunity, then, we understand diversity of provision to meet diverse needs. "Equality of provision," says Tawney, "is to be achieved, not by treating different needs in the same way, but by devoting equal care to ensuring that they are met in the different ways most appropriate to them." This really stands on its head Mill's concept of State direction of education as the inevitable forerunner of uniformity. On this definition, a State education whose aim was to provide real equality of opportunity would seek, not to impose uniformity, but to bring out and develop the latent diversities that cramping social conditions and absence of opportunity have hidden behind a façade of uniformity. The existence and extent of natural inequalities are both irrelevant. What is being attempted is the elimination of *un*natural *in*equalities that limit freedom.

Now this ideal may be, as some believe, a Utopian dream. It must be admitted straight away that we have no guarantees that the attempt will succeed and no precedents on which to base any confident forecasts. Before we try to make up our minds whether we ought to try to achieve it, however, it is worth while remembering that whatever conclusion we come to cannot legitimately claim to be based on the facts, but must inevitably be based on some *a priori* view of human nature, or on judgments regarding the suitability (or the capacity) of the means employed to achieve the end in question, or on doubts regarding the desirability of the end itself. For the facts have not had a long enough trial to justify a conclusion. The experiment has hardly begun. Equality of educational opportunity, to quote merely one instance, is still largely only a paper realization in Great Britain, and this will still be so even if "comprehensive" education becomes the general rule. When the beneficiaries are old enough to make their view known regarding the success of the experiment, we may have more data, not only on education, but on many other facets of the problem, and then, perhaps, we might hazard an argument or two from the facts.

One thing is already clear. To achieve anything like real equality of opportunity will be very difficult. Like all general principles, equality of opportunity is much easier to state in general terms than to work out in practical detail. It is peculiarly difficult because it involves an attempt to recognize at one and the same time two principles that may prove in practice to be in conflict. Equality of opportunity means trying to give every individual as reasonably good a chance as any other. It means treating people as individual cases. But political institutions inevitably have to deal in categories. It is a commonplace that hard cases make bad law. Translated into legislative terms, the principle of equality means that where we can establish a genuine category, when we believe we are really dealing with equals, any obligation that is imposed on one must bear equally on all members of that category. We ought to prohibit night work for all women, or all pregnant women, or even all red-haired women—but not just for Mrs. Smith or Mrs. Jones. If we decide that all children are to stay at school until the age of sixteen, any exceptions to the rule ought to apply again to defined categories. We ought not to exempt John Smith of Barchester because his father works for the Member of Parliament for Barchester, who was at school with the Minister and so persuaded him, for old times sake, to let John leave school at twelve, because his father had a job for him at home.

Yet individual circumstances may be more important in determining opportunities than anything the State can do. We do not know how big a part in individual endowment is played by heredity, about which the best-disposed State can, as yet, do very little. We do not really know what causes some to become geniuses and others criminals, nor why some have the energy and initiative to overcome obstacles unaided, while others, even with help, do not get very far. We do not know much, either, about the diagnosis or the cure of social and psychological maladjustments. Inevitably, both because of our lack of knowledge and also because of our lack of material resources, we are working largely in the dark. We try, by rough and ready methods, to assess people's needs, rather like a sports master making a hurried attempt to handicap the fathers on the field, for a parents' egg and spoon race. The result is that we often seem to be barely scratching the surface of what would have to be done to give real equality of opportunity.

It is partly considerations like these that have led some to conclude that it cannot be done at all, at least not by the State and by the methods that we have tried up to now. In the opinion of some, the remedy for inequality, if there is one, is not political. It is a question of slow evolution, partly moral, through the development of higher personal standards or a more fully developed sense of family responsibility, partly intellectual, through increasing medical, psychological and social knowledge. Others hold that it is possible to remedy social inequality by political means, but not by the particular methods that modern democratic and socially progressive States have adopted. Marxists, as we have already said, argue that we are on the wrong lines altogether. Bernard Shaw had his own theory. He pointed out how difficult it was to find a rational principle of distributing wealth among the different claimants. And he elaborated—and demolished in turn—six principles that had been tried, or could be tried. We could, he said, try to give to each what he or she produces, or deserves, or can get and hold; or we can give the common people enough to keep them alive and the rest to the gentry; or we can distribute wealth by class; or we can go on as we are, muddling along. But the only simple and practicable method, he thought, was to give everybody the same amount. "The only satisfactory plan," he said, "is to give everybody an equal share no matter what sort of person she is, or how old she is, or what sort of work she does, or who or what her father was." "Equal distribution" was also, in his view, "quite possible and practicable, not only momentarily but permanently." And it had "the tremendous advantage of securing promotion by merit for the more capable."[1]

This plan looked simpler to Bernard Shaw than to most of his readers. If it would remove at a blow one source of inequality of opportunity, it would leave plenty of others and create a whole new set of problems as well. It would be to all intents and purposes a revolution, and could probably only be imposed as a result of revolution, with all the hazards and potentialities for misdirection that that implies. It would call for wholesale economic and technical reorganization, probably involving a costly transitional period of dislocation, such as few countries to-day could afford. There are few reasons for believing that social distinctions and snobbery could be so simply and easily eliminated from society. America, which began as a country without an aristocratic caste, and with vast opportunities for citizens with initiative, developed her own social distinctions and inequalities. The most pointed objection to it is that, if it were possible to introduce such a scheme peacefully and smoothly, we should be more than half way to solving the problem of inequality of opportunity without going to all the trouble, for it would already be solved in people's minds. In those circumstances, a number of schemes which now appear to us Utopian might, indeed, begin to look "simple and practicable"!

Of all the "it cannot be done" arguments, perhaps the one that has had most weight is the argument from history. This is often an argument that it *ought* not to be done even if it could. Basically, it is the argument that you cannot change human nature, that there has never been a civilization without gross inequalities of opportunity and that we are going against nature and the lessons of history in trying to create a

---

[1] *The Intelligent Woman's Guide to Socialism and Capitalism* (Constable, 1928), pp. 19, 70.

society in which there is equality of opportunity. It is often urged that progress has always been achieved by intelligent minorities, that throughout history, the mass of human beings have been not leaders, but led, that all the great civilizations, from ancient Athens to eighteenth-century France have been societies in which there was a small and privileged *élite*. If it is true that civilizations advance at the rate determined by the quality of the *élite*, and if, as some claim, the result of equalizing opportunity is to iron out the extremes—to leave us with fewer underdogs but with fewer geniuses as well, to create a dead level of mediocrity—then the result might be to retard the advance of civilization rather than to advance it.

This is the gloomy side of the picture. There are, however, brighter sides. The argument from history can cut both ways. The fact that it has never been done proves nothing, for history is full of examples to prove that everything has had to be done a first time. Moreover, the argument from *élites* has a recoil. The ideas that we have been studying in this book have often been fought for, and died for, by men who had no hope of seeing victory within their own generation, or for many generations to come. Some of them belonged themselves to the *élite* whose privileged position they were seeking to destroy. Some were fighting systems and ideas that were firmly established, not only in their own countries, but almost throughout the civilized world.

Nor is the argument that the task is heartbreakingly difficult any more conclusive. The French have a saying that "in politics, everything is always very difficult indeed." Few of the liberties that we enjoy to-day were won easily. Some required centuries of struggle. The effective battle for equality only really began with the French and American revolutions. The real battle for equality of economic opportunity—as distinct from the isolated efforts of earlier pioneers—does not go back much more than a generation. If we look back at the conditions that prevailed a century ago, it seems to many observers that the progress that has been made not only justifies the attempt and gives reasonable hope of success, but calls for some acceleration of the present rate of advance.

All the same, it would be unwise to underestimate the difficulties, difficulties both of attaining reasonable equality of opportunity and of attaining it at a price that we feel is worth paying. Whether we accept or reject the view that increasing equality will bring us greater freedom will probably depend more than anything else on our individual standards of values. But even if we believe that equality and liberty need not be incompatible, it by no means follows that they *must* be compatible. The answer to the question: Are liberty and equality compatible? may be one that it is within our power to answer only by our acts. We said at the outset of this enquiry that the citizen is not only the product of his history, but the maker of it. The answer may depend on whether or not we decide, either as citizens, or as a civilization, to *make* liberty and equality compatible. Or to put it differently, the answer may depend both on the quality of the opportunity that we strive to recognize and on the quality of our citizenship. We have seen that the extension of rights involves, necessarily and inevitably, an extension of concomitant duties. If liberty is, as we defined it at the beginning of this chapter, a "system of harmonized liberties" (or rights), then the increase *pari passu* of rights and duties could certainly diminish freedom. It all depends on the ways in which men use the potentialities set free by the extension of rights. If, too, as we saw earlier in this chapter, the principle of equality ceases to be used as a touchstone, by which we can measure the extent to which others are enjoying real moral freedom, and is misused as a measuring rod to enable us to see that our neighbour never has a fraction more of anything than we have, then we may, like the Icarians, lose sight of liberty.

The association of men in the State will always be bound to raise many difficult problems. We have tried to indicate some of them, to analyse the points at issue and to describe some of the solutions that have been put forward from time to time. We have tried, however, as far as is humanly possible, to leave the reader free to come to his own conclusions, without having the writer's own private views flung at his head at every turn. For if the problems are to be solved, it will only be on the basis of solutions provided by and accepted by the citizen. Whether they will be good or bad solutions will depend on the quality of the effort that the individual citizen is willing to make, in order to think out the problems of government, as they need to be thought out afresh in every generation.

In his task, the citizen will be carrying on the work of past generations of history makers. His attempts to work out the twentieth century implications of the rights to liberty, equality, or happiness will owe much to those men who have tried to do for their own time what he is trying to do for his; to men like Pym, Hampden, Burke, Wilkes, Fox, Pitt, Bradlaugh, who fought for the rights or enhanced the prestige of the Parliament of this country; to thinkers like Locke, Bentham, Rousseau, Mill, Proudhon or Marx, who tried to think out the principles of government; to a host of past and present political leaders and, finally, to a host of unknown people who, like himself, tried to work out where they stood on the burning issues of the day. It is essential to good government that the succession should be uninterrupted. "For freedom, we know, is a thing that we have to conquer afresh for ourselves, every day, like love. . . . The battle of freedom is never done, and the field never quiet."

Appendix

LIST OF BOOKS FOR FURTHER READING

I. BACKGROUND STUDIES ON POLITICS AND POLITICAL THEORY

T. D. Weldon, *States and Morals*, John Murray, 1947.

E. F. Carritt, *Morals and Politics*, Oxford University Press, 1935.

J. D. Mabbott, *The State and the Citizen*, Hutchinson's University Library, 1949.

R. H. S. Crossman, *Government and the Governed*, Chatto and Windus, 1969.

Maurice Cranston (Ed.), *A Glossary of Political Terms*, Bodley Head, 1966.

David Thomson (Ed.), *Political Ideas*, Watts, 1966.

Maurice Duverger, *The Idea of Politics*, Methuen, 1966.

Bernard Crick, *In Defence of Politics*, Weidenfeld and Nicolson, 1962.

Michael Oakeshott, *Social and Political Doctrines of Contemporary Europe*, Oxford University Press, 1950.
Rationalism in Politics, Methuen, 1962.

J. D. B. Miller, *The Nature of Politics*, Duckworth, 1962.

II. THE STATE

H. J. Laski, *The State in Theory and Practice*, Allen and Unwin, 1935.

R. M. MacIver, *The Web of Government*, Macmillan, 1948.
The Modern State, Oxford Paperbacks, 1964.

Ernest Barker, *Principles of Social and Political Theory*, Oxford Paperbacks, 1961.

III. DEMOCRACY AND REVOLUTION

D. Thomson, *The Democratic Ideal in France and England*, Cambridge University Press, 1940.

C. K. Allen, *Democracy and the Individual*, Oxford University Press, 1943.

H. B. Mayo, *An Introduction to Democratic Theory*, Oxford University Press, 1960.

H. R. G. Greaves, *The Foundation of Political Theory*, Allen and
  Unwin, 1958.
J. L. Talmon, *The Origins of Totalitarian Democracy*, Mercury
  Books, 1961.
Herbert Agar, *The Perils of Democracy*, Bodley Head, 1965.
C. B. Macpherson, *The Real World of Democracy*, Oxford,
  1966.
Karl Marx and Frederick Engels, *Manifesto of the Communist
  Party*, Martin Lawrence, 1934.
V. I. Lenin, *State and Revolution*, Little Lenin Library, Vol. 14,
  1933.
D. W. Brogan, *The Price of Revolution*, Hamish Hamilton, 1951.
G. B. Shaw, *Essays in Fabian Socialism*, Constable, 1932.
Leonard Schapiro, *Totalitarianism*, Pall Mall Press, 1972.
Dorothy Pickles, *Democracy*, Methuen, 1971.

IV. INTERNATIONAL PROBLEMS

Elie Kedourie, *Nationalism*, Hutchinson's University Library,
  1961.
Geoffrey Goodwin, *Britain and the United Nations*, Oxford
  University Press, 1958.
H. G. Nicholas, *The United Nations as a Political Institution*,
  Oxford Paperbacks, 1962.
Max Beloff, *Europe and the Europeans*, Chatto and Windus, 1957.
Walter Kolarz, *Communism and Colonialism*, Macmillan, 1964.
K. R. Minogue, *Nationalism*, Batsford, 1967.
Douglas Evans (Ed.), *Destiny or Delusion—Britain and the Com-
  mon Market*, Gollancz, 1971.
        Britain in the E.E.C., Gollancz, 1973.
F. S. Northedge (Ed.), *The Foreign Policies of the Powers*, Faber
  and Faber, 1974.

V. RIGHTS, DUTIES, LIBERTY AND EQUALITY

L. T. Hobhouse, *The Elements of Social Justice*, Allen and Unwin,
  1921.
H. J. Laski, *Liberty in the Modern State*, Faber and Faber, 1930.

Maurice Cranston, *Human Rights Today*, Ampersand Books, 1962.
———— *Freedom*, Longmans, 1954.
R. H. Tawney, *Equality*, Allen and Unwin, 1931.
A. P. d'Entrèves, *Natural Law*, Hutchinson's University Library, 1951.
Charles Howard McIlwain, *Constitutionalism: Ancient and Modern*, Great Seal Books, Cornell University Press, 1947.

VI. SOME POLITICAL THEORISTS

Plato, *The Republic of Plato*, Cornford, Oxford University Press, 1945.
Aristotle, *Politics*, Ernest Barker Ed., Oxford University Press, 1947.
Thomas Hobbes, *Leviathan* (Introduction by Michael Oakshott), Blackwell, 1957.
John Locke, *Of Civil Government*, in *Social Contract*, World's Classics, Oxford University Press, 1948.
Jean-Jacques Rousseau, *Social Contract*, also in above.
John Stuart Mill, *Utilitarianism*, *Liberty* and *Representative Government*, Everyman's Library, Dent, 1926.
  Autobiography, World's Classics, Oxford University Press, 1924.

On the above, see also:—
Ernest Barker, *Greek Political Theory*, Methuen, University Paperbacks, 1960.
H. J. Laski, *From Locke to Bentham*, Home University Library, 1920.
Peter Laslett, *John Locke, Two Treatises of Government*, Cambridge University Press, 1960.
John Plamenatz, *The English Utilitarians*, Blackwell, 1958.
  Man and Society (2 vols.), Longmans, 1963.
C. E. Vaughan, *The Political Writings of Rousseau* (2 vols.), Blackwell, 1962.

Index

Acton, Lord, 30, 199, 210
Africa, 122, 123, 126
Alice Through the Looking-Glass, 91
Alsace and Lorraine, 35
American Declaration of Independence (1776), 72, 151–153
Aristotle, 16, 17, 58, 98, 137
Atlantic Charter (1941), 154
Austin, John, 61

Bagehot, Walter, 28, 81n
Balfour, Lord, 81, 95
Basques, 36
Beard. C. and M., 160
Belgium, 43, 55
Benelux, 120
Bentham, Jeremy, 76–78, 79, 80, 82, 137, 217
Benthamism, 86
Bingo, 180
Blum, Léon, 88
Bradlaugh, Charles, 217
Britain, *see under* Great Britain
British Dominions, 35
Burke, Edmund, 61, 217

Cabet, Etienne, 209
Can Parliament Survive?, 103
Carritt, E. F., 75n
Catherine of Russia, 162
Catholics, 51–52
Catlin, George, 30n
Cecil, Lord Hugh, 188
Character, national, 23–25
Christian Scientists, 47
Clootz, Anacharsis, 26
Cole, G. D. H., 143, 147, 179
Commonwealth, 124, 132
Communism (ists), 47, 85, 97, 100, 105, 117, 122, 125–126, 132, 188; and democracy, 94, 96

Communist China, 99, 123, 129
Community sense, development of, 144–145
Congo, 118, 130
Conscientious objection, 47, 55, 92–93, 196
Conservative Party, 34, 172
Conservatives, 21, 188
Contract, Social, 62–72, 153
Council of Europe, 117, 120, 164, 167, 168
Crossman, R. H. S., 20, 24n, 88n
Cuba, 118, 128
Cypriots, 36, 118
Czechs, 36

D'Anglas, Boissy, 26
Davis, Garry, 36
Deakin, Arthur, 94, 96
De la Rivière, Mercier, 162
Democracy, 200; revolutionary movements in a, 91–100; changes in, 100–102; improvement in techniques of, 102–108
Dicey, A. V., 42
Divine right, doctrine of, 60, 63, 64

Education, 176, 189, 211–212
Education and equality, 211
Equality, 45–46, 72–73, 76–77, 82, 152, 154, 156, 160, 199–200; French emphasis on, 199; economic, 201; different meanings of, 207–216
European Coal and Steel Community, 24, 116, 124
European Coal Commission, 121
European Convention of Human Rights, 164–167, 168, 169, 170
European Defence Community, 116
European Economic Community, 69, 119, 120, 124, 131–133

222

Index

FABIANISM, 105–106
Fascism, 100
Feudalism, 64
Fifth French Republic, 105, 118, 156, 159, 162, 164, 182
Filmer, Sir Robert, 60
Fourier, Charles, 209
Fourth French Republic, 40, 159, 162, 182
Fox, C. J., 217
France, 24–25, 26, 32, 49, 89–90, 116–118, 123, 128, 132, 215; Communist Party, 32, 118; Constitutions, 43, 156, 160, 162, 164, 182; freedom in, 50, 52, 54, 55; and the State, 52; tolerance of para-military groups, 96, 97; syndicalism in, 105; rights in, 159; constitutional changes, 163–164
French Revolution, 85, 86, 88, 90; Declaration of the Rights of Man, 72, 151–153, 156
Freedom, individual, 48, 49–53. *See also under* Liberty
Friends, Society of, 47, *see also under* Quakers
Full employment, policy of, 185–186

Gaullism, 119
General will, theory of, 70–75, 77
Germany, 86, 105, 115, 129; Weimar Republic, 40; Hegel and, 73–74
Government, distinguished from the State, 34–35
Great Britain, 24–25, 27, 34, 85, 92, 99, 118, 123, 137, 143, 191, 197; Dicey on sovereignty in, 42; effects of industrial revolution, 49; Catholics in, 51, 52; and the State, 52; Trade Unionism, 52–53; individual freedom in, 53, 54,

55; majority system in, 81; re-voluntary minorities in, 97; citizen's rights in, 156–157, 158; Constitution, 161, 163–164
Green, T. H., 74
Grotius, Hugo, 111

HAGUE Tribunal, 112–113
Hammond, J. L. and B., 50n
Hampden, John, 217
Happiness, 72–73, 152; Bentham and, 76–78, 80
Hawtrey, R. G., 132n
Hegel, G. W. F., 73–74
Hitler, A., 41, 47, 117
Hobbes, Thomas, 22, 59, 65, 68, 69
Hobhouse, L. T., 150, 171, 171n, 198
Hogg, Quintin, 21
Hollis, Christopher, 103
Hume, David, 61
Hungary, 117

INDIA, 123
International Army proposal, 116
International Labour Office, 120
International organization, efforts to set up, 109–114; essential weaknesses of, 114–117; functional agencies, 119–125; and human rights, 164–170
International Telegraphic Union, 120
Ireland (Northern), 32
Israel, 36, 117, 209n
Italy, 86, 105, 115, 132

JENKS, E., 39n
Jews, 36
Johnson, Samuel, 61

KANT, Immanuel, 61, 112
Korea, invasion of. 31, 110

LAMENNAIS, Félicité Robert de, 141
Laski, Harold, 22, 31, 32, 34, 39, 40, 46, 47, 85, 95, 96, 97, 145
Laws of Peace and War, The, 111
League of Nations, 113-114, 115, 116, 120
Lenin, V.I., 40, 90
Levellers, 187
Liberal Party, 34
Liberty, 152, 153, 154, 155, 160; and duties, 198-199; Anglo-Saxon emphasis on, 199; Marxist view of, 201; Mill on, 202-207
Lindsay, A. D., 74
Local government, 142, 147
Locke, John, 22, 23, 60, 63, 65-69, 70, 71, 153, 157, 188, 217
Louis XIV, King of France, 41, 47
Louis XV, King of France, 69

MABBOTT, J. D., 56n, 151n
MacIver, R. M., 31, 34, 37, 45, 57, 84, 96
Maine, Sir Henry, 61
Managerial Revolution, The, 102
Marshall Aid, 122
Martin, Kingsley, 23n
Martineau, Harriet, 189
Marx, Karl, 17, 19-20, 22, 45-46, 50, 62, 82, 90, 180, 217
Marxism, 25, 46, 62, 98-99, 100, 107, 201, 210, 213
Mill, John Stuart, 55, 77, 80, 202-207, 211, 217
Minorities, problem of, 80-82, 92-98
Montesquieu, C. L. de Secondat, 46, 111
More, Hannah, 49
Mormons, 87
Mussolini, B., 105

NATION, concept of, 35-36
North Atlantic Treaty Alliance, 129
National Coal Board, 145

National Health Service, 175, 178-179, 191
Nationalist China, 130
Nationality, 36
Nationalization, 106
Nazism, 41
Norway, 54

ORWELL, George, 48
Owen, Robert, 209
Organization for Economic Co-operation and Development, 120

PACIFISM(ISTS), 111-112, 196
Paley, Archdeacon, 60
Penn, William, 111
Pitt, William ("the Elder"), 18
Pitt, William ("the Younger"), 217
Plato, 16, 17, 59, 68
Popular sovereignty, doctrine of, 43-45
Power, use by Governments, 40-41; limits to, 42-43, 46-51; economic and political, 45-46; Marx's view of, 45-46; safeguards against domination by one organ, 46
Property, private, 65, 152, 153, 155, 157-158, 160, 188-189, 208-209
Proudhon, Pierre Joseph, 217
Psycho-analysis, 25
Pym, John, 217

QUAKERS, 75

RATIONALISM, 25-26
Representation, functional, 103-105
Revolution, meaning of, 84-86; causes of, 86-87; dangers and difficulties of, 88-91; moral argument against, 91; in a democratic state, 91-98; Marxist view of, 98-100
Rights, moral and legal, 150; theoretical and enforceable, 150-151; "natural", 151-168; in

American and French Constitutions, 151–153; fundamental rights to-day, 154–169; discrepancies between theory and practice, 158–162, 164; and duties, 170–173, 175–197
Rousseau, Jean-Jacques, 17, 23, 69–71, 73, 208, 209, 217
Russia, 49, 50, 90, 97, 99, 115, 117, 123, 128–131, 155, 160, 196; and Declaration of Human Rights, 155
Russian Revolution, 85, 86, 88, 90

Scots, 35
Shaw, G. B., 182, 189, 191, 204–205, 213–214
Smith, Adam, 73
Socialism, 137; and functional representation, 105–106
Social services, 175–180, 181, 182, 188–193
South Africa, 32, 54
South America, revolutions in, 86
Sovereignty, legal and political, 42–43; popular, doctrine of, 43–45; checks and balances, 46; Laski on, 46–47
Soviet Russia, *see under* Russia
Spain, 36, 40, 105, 115
Stalin, J., 90
State, nature of, 34–39; sovereign power of, 39–40, 41; limit to its power, 42–43, 46–51; Marx's view of, 45–46, 50; problem of reasonable limits on, 54–56; obedience to, 57–83; contract theories, 62–72; modern citizen's dependence on, 175, 181
Stawell, F. Melian, 111
Stephen, Leslie, 22, 42

Strikes, 53, 159, 182, 183–184
Sudeten Germans, 36
Suez, 118
Switzerland, (*and* the Swiss), 32, 35, 43
Syndicalism, 105, 107

Tawney, R. H., 211
Thorez, Maurice, 97
Trade Unions, 155, 165, 181, 182; and the State, 51, 52–53
Tunisia, 118, 123

United Nations Organization, 110, 114, 115, 117, 120, 121, 127, 129–130, 154, 155
U.S.A., 27, 28, 32, 35, 54, 55, 132, 159–160, 162–163, 214
Universal Declaration of Human Rights, 154, 164, 165–166
Universal Postal Union, 120
Universal suffrage, 101
Utilitarianism, 76–77, 78

Voluntary associations, 143
Vyshinsky, A., 155

War, attempts to prevent by international authority, 109–115, 127–134; modern war and the citizen, 194–197; nuclear war, 128, 180, 195–197
Webb, Sydney and Beatrice, 103
Weldon, T. D., 59
Wells, H. G., 103
Welsh nationality, 35
Wilkes, John, 217
Work, right to, 181–188